PREMEDITATED SELLING

Tools for Developing the **Right** Strategy
for **Every** Opportunity

ASTD
PRESS

ignite
Sales Simulations that Inspire

…ielda and **Kevin Jones**

ASTD Press is an internationally renowned source of insightful and practical information on workplace learning and performance topics, including training basics, evaluation and return-on-investment, instructional systems development, e-learning, leadership, and career development.

Ordering information: Books published by ASTD Press can be purchased by visiting ASTD's website at store.astd.org or by calling 800.628.2783 or 703.683.8100.

Library of Congress Control Number: 2012940628

ISBN-10: 1-56286-844-6
ISBN-13: 978-1-56286-844-4

ASTD Press Editorial Staff:
Director: Glenn Saltzman
Community of Practice Manager, Sales Enablement: Mike Galvin
Associate Editor: Stephanie Castellano
Design and Production: Lon Levy
Cover Design: Ana Foreman

Printed by Versa Press, Inc., East Peoria, IL, www.versapress.com

Contents

Preface

We have been working with sales leaders in Fortune 1000 companies for more than 15 years. During that time alone there have been many books written on strategic account management and many training programs developed with the intent of helping salespeople become more effective when working with their top accounts. A few years ago, we were working with the vice president of sales at a large Fortune 1000 company. This person told us that he needed a way to help make the company's strategic account management process more actionable. He wanted a way to help his team think and act strategically. He wanted his team to be more proactive in analyzing the multiple opportunities within a single account and be smarter in the way they put together a strategy to win the business. This VP needed his team to be able to use the strategic account management process in a way that would help them determine where they should invest time, who they should invest time with, and which strategy would best demonstrate the company's ability to help their customers achieve their business outcomes.

We assumed that since this company had already implemented a reputable strategic account management process, they had every tool they needed to be successful. Unfortunately, we were wrong. Instead the "process" being implemented inside this company was seen by the sales force as nothing more than forms, unnecessary paperwork. And while these forms were excellent repositories of information, they did little to change the way the salespeople approached their business.

The sad reality is that this company, and its VP of sales, aren't alone. In fact, there are many companies, of all shapes and sizes, implementing strategic account management processes without achieving the intended results. Our experiences with many other Fortune 1000 companies have revealed that many salespeople are *not* using their strategic account management process to think and act more strategically when working with their top accounts. Instead, they are merely filling out forms believing they are being strategic in their approach, and unfortunately, their sales managers are encouraging that behavior.

Our experiences with top-performing salespeople show that they know how to think and act strategically. Top performers are more intentional in their strategic account planning and meditate on their approach before acting. Top performers don't just collect data and fill out forms, they know what data to collect and what actions need to be taken to successfully leverage that data. This book has been written to help you become more actionable, intentional—more "premeditated"—in the way you approach every sales opportunity.

This book provides you with a set of tools to help you organize critical opportunity data and ideas for how to use that data in developing an opportunity strategy. We broke this book into five segments that are fundamental to any sales strategy. Within these segments we identify the types of information any seller needs, provide tools to organize the information, and ideas to analyze the information and develop a path forward. Each of the segments, although independent of each other, work together to provide a complete plan for a sales opportunity. These tools work. We've used them and our customers have used them. Approaching any sales opportunity without them is like taking a long drive without a map.

While this book is intended for salespeople and sales leaders, those individuals aren't the only ones who can benefit from the application of the concepts. Knowing how to develop the right strategy for every opportunity isn't going to just help a salesperson win more deals, it is going to help the business manage critical functions that rely so heavily on accurate sales forecasting. Operations will have a better sense for planning, finance will have a better handle on future cash flow. Deals that inexplicably move from "won" to "lost" don't just impact the salesperson's commission—they impact the way businesses run.

"There are plenty of books on sales strategy but very few that are as useful as this one. I greatly respect Steve and Kevin's contribution."

NEIL RACKHAM
Executive Professor of Professional Selling
University of Cincinnati
Author of the classic *SPIN Selling*

Acknowledgments

We had a lot of fun writing this book and we are grateful for our many customers that provided us with valuable cases studies: Boston Scientific, Time Warner, Kimberly Clark, Booz Allen Hamilton, CR Bard, MasterCard, Weight Watchers, Lumenis, and others. These customers shared awesome examples of both the right ways and the not-so-right ways to approach strategy. We want to thank them for sharing their trials and tribulations with us and for letting us tell their stories.

Although this book was a lot of fun, it was also a lot of hard work. Stories had to be written and rewritten, models had be created and then re-created. We are fortunate to have colleagues that helped analyze and critique our ideas. We'd like to offer special thanks to Scott Pierce, Neil Rackham, Dick Ruff, Janet Spirer, Pam Weber, Bill Schnitzer, Dave Roberts, Robin Dogas, Paul Menichelli, and Bob DiSilvio.

And of course we couldn't and wouldn't have done this with the blessing of our families. We want to offer up our sincere thanks to Sherry and Kayla Gielda, and Donna, Aidan, and Poppy Jones. We know this book took time away from you that can't be replaced. We'd also like to extend a special thanks to Richard Gielda, Stacy Gielda, and Bob Jones for their support and encouragement and for acting as a sounding board for our ideas.

Chapter 1

Thinking and Acting Strategically

A darkened plane at 35,000 feet—a late-night flight home from a tough client meeting—is a great place to reflect. And on this flight, there is a lot to reflect on. A deal had been lost. This opportunity had seemed a sure thing, a sure thing that was now dead. Why? A mental post-mortem of any sales opportunity is—or ought to be—inevitable, especially for an opportunity that slid inexplicably from the "won" to the "lost" column. Questions of what could have been will haunt your thoughts. What was missed? Was the pricing model off? Did a key influencer get overlooked? Was my competitor's solution really better than mine? Ultimately, salespeople on the losing side are desperate to know why their opportunity went south.

And You Think You Lost Because of *Price*?

Although much has changed in the field of sales during the two decades we've been in this business, one element that hasn't changed is a salesperson's readiness to blame a lost opportunity on price. In our years as sales performance consultants, we have asked salespeople the following question countless times: "Why do you think the customer selected your competitor?" By far, the number one response to this question is "price." It may be phrased in a number of ways, but the crux of the message is, "I couldn't create enough value for my customer to select my solution over other less costly alternatives." Ironically, although price is the reason sellers most commonly give for losing a deal, it is seldom the reason customers give for choosing the competition.

Just recently, we were working with the sales team of a large software company. Part of our project was to evaluate lost opportunities in hopes of finding out what was going wrong. Salespeople inside this organization clearly felt that the majority of deals lost were due to noncompetitive pricing. In fact, in the evaluation of these lost opportunities, salespeople blamed price for the loss in more than 75 percent of the cases. In post-mortem interviews with clients, however, we heard a different story. Not only was price *not* the number one reason customers chose an alternative solution; price didn't even make their top three. Instead, customers provided other reasons for selecting alternative solutions, such as not being comfortable with the company's level of post-sales support, the lack of efficacy data for the product, the ease of use or training curve of implementing the new product, and so forth. The fact that price was rarely mentioned as a deciding factor came as a surprise to the salespeople who had worked with these customers. How could they have overlooked the real reasons their customers went with the competition?

The sad truth for our client—and for many sellers on the losing side— is that there was little understanding of the buying process the client was going to use, who was going to be involved in the process, and which factors were going to be important when evaluating alternatives. What do you do in the absence of good information? You make assumptions about what's important and why. Sellers will approach clients by emphasizing product strengths and attributes that they believe are important. They will anticipate issues and challenges that have presented themselves before. Sometimes a salesperson will get lucky in this method and hit his mark, but more often, he will not. Acting on assumptions, letting history solely influence your approach—in short, depending on luck, makes for a pretty poor sales strategy.

Getting Ahead of the Curve

With enough analysis, and the right customer resource, any salesperson can uncover the real reason an opportunity went south. Unfortunately, having this knowledge doesn't change anything—the deal is done, and you came out on the losing end. But wouldn't it be nice to have known the reasons you lost before the deal was actually over? If you had known you were in a losing position, what would you have done differently? The process we provide in this book, when used appropriately, can minimize the need for lost opportunity post-mortems by helping you win more and lose less. It will help you understand where you stand in the eyes of the customer, by highlighting your strengths and revealing your vulnerabilities. Gaining this insight allows you to act before it's too late. And while the information you procure may prompt you to take a variety of actions, from modifying call points, to bringing in additional resources, or simply walking away, it is this ability to act on good information that will alter your outcomes.

One Word—Strategery

During the 2000 United States presidential election, Will Ferrell performed exceptional impersonations of George W. Bush on *Saturday Night Live*. During one such performance, Ferrell's character was asked to sum up his presidential campaign in one word. Ferrell's response was as memorable as it was brief—"strategery." As laughable as the word is, it may just be the best summation of the process many salespeople employ when approaching major sales opportunities. Many salespeople spend time gathering account information; they then put that information into a company-mandated account strategy "form," and then they sit through an agonizing meeting that management often calls an "account planning session." Unfortunately, these meetings are more like an interrogation of the sales rep so that the manager can be brought up to speed on the account. There is very little value created by this process—this is strategery.

What Does "Premeditated Selling" Mean?

We struggled in coming up with a title for this book that would reflect the value of the solution we present inside its covers. We asked ourselves countless times, "What is it that we hope people will do differently after reading this book?" The answer is simple. We want people to give more forethought to how they manage a sales opportunity. We want them to develop more proactive strategies that will help create opportunities for success. There were a lot of terms we could have used in our title, but we settled on *premeditated* because of its direct meaning—"to meditate, consider, or plan beforehand." Putting aside the term's association with well-planned crime, the definition was an exact description of what top salespeople do when working on an important sales opportunity—they meditate, consider, and plan beforehand.

A Premeditated Selling Process

This book will show you how to develop a sales plan for each unique opportunity inside your accounts, using a five-step process that has proven itself successful. This process evaluates a sales opportunity from various angles, providing you insight into your situation and ideas for moving forward. Each step provides tools to help you analyze an opportunity and gather the information you need to make your next move. The five steps of the Premeditated Selling Process are:

1. Understanding the buying factors

2. Leveraging the key players

3. Optimizing the buying environment

4. Influencing the competitive landscape

5. Quantifying the value of your solution

Step 1—Understanding the buying factors: the analysis of the buying process your customer will use for making their purchasing decision. By understanding how your customer will actually make their decision, you can modify the speed with which you act, the resources you use, and the strengths you present. We'll explore this topic a bit further in chapter 2. We'll challenge you to think about the answers to questions like:

- How has the buying process for similar products gone in the past? Is it a consistent process?

- What is the sense of urgency driving your customer's buying process?

- Is there a need for consensus among the decision makers or is diversity of opinion okay?

In today's market we must be able to answer these questions plus many others regarding our customers' buying factors.

Step 2—Leveraging the key players: the analysis of the individuals involved in the buying process—their influence and their perceptions of potential solution providers. By gaining insight into your advocates and adversaries, including who they support and why, you can develop a plan of action to capitalize on your positive relationships while minimizing potential threats. In chapter 3, we're going to take a deeper dive and provide you with a tool that will help you better analyze the key influencers in every sales opportunity. We'll challenge you to think about the answers to questions like:

- What's been said or done to make you believe your advocate is really your advocate?

- Is there a way to leverage your advocates to neutralize your adversaries? If so, how can that be done?

- Who are your competitors' advocates? Are they the same as yours?

We'll help you better analyze all the key influencers involved in your opportunity so you can develop a smart strategy to leverage advocate support.

Step 3—Optimizing the buying environment: the analysis of the trends in your customer's industry and how they affect your customer, specifically the executives inside your customer's organization. By evaluating what's happening in your customer's world, you can anticipate unique challenges and prepare yourself to address needs that your competitors may not have considered. In chapter 4, we'll introduce you to a model that will help you think about how a single trend in the market impacts the customers in your territory; and more importantly, how it changes the way your customer makes purchasing decisions. We're going to challenge you to think about:

- Which market trends are having the greatest impact on this customer? How will they affect your sales efforts?

- What new initiatives has this account taken to leverage or combat these new trends?

- What responsibility do these stakeholders have to help their company take advantage of or combat the trends in the market?

This chapter contains two case studies that reveal best practices for reacting to your customer's buying environment, and show you how to avoid the common traps salespeople often fall into in this part of the sales planning process.

Step 4—Influencing the competitive landscape: the analysis of your competitive position through an understanding of what selection criteria your customer will use and how they compare you to the competitive alternatives. By thinking broadly about the criteria a customer will use to make a decision and knowing your strengths and weaknesses against those criteria, you can develop a strategy to capitalize on your strengths and minimize your weaknesses. In chapter 5, we're going to challenge you to reassess your understanding of your customer's decision criteria. You'll be prompted to consider questions such as:

- Who have you spoken with to confirm the customer's selection criteria?

- If there are multiple decision makers, do they all agree on the same selection criteria? Whose selection criteria matters most and why?

- How does the customer perceive your ability to meet their needs?

Step 5—Quantifying the value of your solution: the analysis of your solution's "value," which enables you to position your solution effectively. By using the classic value equation, you can develop a strategy to build economic value, either through actual or conceptual benefits. In chapter 6, we're going to stretch your thinking around how your customer measures value. We're going to push you to think about:

- What are the most important business outcomes your customer will receive by implementing your solution?

- How will your customer measure your solution's value?

- What metrics have you chosen to measure the value impact of the outcomes?

All too often salespeople underestimate the importance of quantifying the value of their solution. They assume the customer can make the connection between their solution and the impact it can have on the customer's metrics. Unfortunately, these kinds of assumptions can make the difference between winning or losing the opportunity.

Chapter 7 explores the importance of aligning your pipeline or funnel management system to your Premeditated Selling Process. Too often steps are skipped accidentally or maybe even on purpose. Establishing strategic milestones along the way will help both you and your manager know what's happening in the account and which critical next steps need to be taken to move the sales process forward in your favor.

Chapter 8 is dedicated to sales managers. We know that managing a sales team in today's market isn't easy. You are being pulled in many different directions. You're asked to help close this deal, help put out this fire, and to be sure you have your weekly or monthly reports in on time. The list of things you must do never seems to end. So how in the world do you have time to help your team to think and act more strategically with their top opportunities? In this chapter, we're going to provide you with a simple six-step strategic coaching process that will help you guide your sales reps in developing initial strategic opportunity plans. We've included a list of strategic coaching questions that every manager should be asking their sales reps. We hope this chapter provides you with the additional tools needed to help your team win more deals.

Getting Started

Common sense should tell you that you need to develop a strategy before you begin to implement it. If not, it would be like the proverbial "cart before the horse." But developing a strategy sounds akin to planning, which many people equate to paperwork, and we don't know many salespeople who even remotely like paperwork. Filling out forms and reports can feel like a waste of time; and indeed, it does keep sellers from really crucial sales activities, like actually talking to customers. Is it any wonder so many salespeople shrink from formal planning processes?

It is our intention to help you think differently about strategic opportunity planning. Ease of use and immediate relevancy should characterize all sales planning efforts. With this in mind, we have designed tools to walk you through the five steps of the Premeditated Selling Process. These tools provide a framework for consistency, so that sales planning processes are repeatable and information can be shared across an enterprise in a commonly understood way. As you complete these tools, they may reveal gaps in your knowledge about your accounts, which are then up to you to fill. A well-designed tool can enable you to evaluate a situation and organize your information. But it's what you do with the information that matters.

The premeditated approach to selling that we present in this book won't win you every opportunity that comes your way. But it'll help you win more of them. And if you lose, you are equipped to uncover the real reasons why—information that can empower you to win the next one around—instead of defaulting to the infamous excuse of pricing.

Chapter 2

Understanding Buying Factors

Nick Marshall is a Chicago advertising executive with a gift. It's not necessarily a creative gift, but it is one which helps him be creative. Nick can read women's thoughts. Really. It seems he was slightly electrocuted, which hyper-sensitized his cognitive synapses, or something like that. The result is that the female mind is open to him. One does not need much imagination to speculate about the sorts of adventures such a gift would cause. But one may need a fairly strong memory to remember that Nick Marshall is a figment of Patrick Swidler's and Josh Goldsmith's imaginations. Nick is a character they created in their screenplay for the film *What Women Want* and he was portrayed by the then-uncontroversial Mel Gibson.

However the artistic merits of the film may be considered (it scored 54 percent on Rotten Tomatoes' Tomatometer), its plot poses an interesting dilemma. Have you ever really wondered what it would be like to read other people's minds? It might be as much of a curse as a blessing (as Nick discovered when he had the gift). On the other hand, success in major account, complex sales may be more easily come by if you could just get inside your customers' heads to know what they're thinking. What do they want, and why do they want it?

While this book will not grant you the ability to read your customers' minds, it will shed light on what your customers are thinking as they make their buying decisions. Let's begin by exploring five critical factors underlying the customer's buying process. The first component of thinking and acting strategically is understanding these five factors (shown in the figure on the next page).

Marathon or Sprint? The Length of the Decision Process

"Hurry up and wait" is a proverb born of the military world, where the need to be constantly ready often leads to hurried preparations followed by extended periods of idle waiting. Constant preparedness in the military is necessary, as the consequences of not being ready are severe and life threatening. But "hurry up and wait" in selling is a recipe for frustration and failure, as well as an indication that the

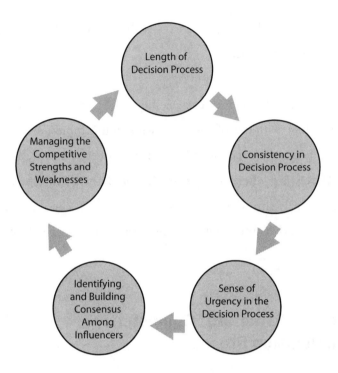

sales strategy has gone awry. The first factor contributing to a success-ful strategy, then, has to do with knowing how long it's going to take for the customer to decide.

Just as a marathon consumes the runner's energy over a long period, so a lengthy decision cycle consumes the seller's resources. The seller needs to pace himself in order to have enough energy for the end of the race. A lengthy cycle requires equal parts patience and persistence. The seller needs to stay connected to her advocates, to keep her fingers on the customer's pulse, and to watch for signs of change. The savvy seller also needs to keep his resources at the ready, held in reserve for the final kick at the finish.

On the other hand, a shorter cycle is more like a sprint. It's all muscle and adrenaline, with lots of energy consumed in a rapid burst. Finishing a sprint demands that the seller align resources as quickly as possible, and know just when to use them. Too often the average performer will haphazardly throw resources, such as research, client references, and senior sales executives into the sales process in a desperate attempt to win the sale.

Same Old, Same Old? Consistency of the Decision Process

We have a friend who recently toured Ireland. He had hired a car in Dublin with plans to drive to Belfast. When it came time to refuel, he did what he always did in the States: He pulled into the service station, pulled up to the pump, and filled his tank. He paid and drove off, on the left side of the road, naturally. A few kilometers from the station, he and his car shared an amazing discovery: Petroleum will not power a diesel engine. His car died—sputtered and died as though it had run out of fuel, which in a way, it had. Fortunately for our friend, he was able to call upon a local business that rescues drivers in this circumstance for a modest fee (and we suppose, with discretion).

We can all learn a lesson from our friend's experience: Just because we have done something the same way for years does not mean it will always be that way. We find that successful salespeople test their assumptions about how a normally familiar process will flow for each opportunity. They take nothing for granted. All the old familiar faces may still be in place, but perhaps they will have different influences on each decision. While a formal request for proposal (RFP) process may be the norm for one of your accounts, does that mean there will be one for every opportunity inside it? What cast of characters will make up your competition? What do they bring to the table this time?

If you approach a new opportunity with old eyes you run the risk of looking unsophisticated or just plain lazy in the eyes of your customer. And unfortunately, there is no "sales rescue" company that will save your deal.

While working with a major consumer packaged goods company that is focused in frozen foods, we had the great pleasure of working with Peter, a top-performing sales rep with 15 years' experience in the industry. Peter had been working hard to expand his company's share of shelf space within a large national grocery chain. His competitor, however, was king in this specific product category in all the chain's stores across the country. Both Peter and his competitor understood that the customer was interested in improving its revenues in this specific frozen food category. They both developed a compelling argument that they each deserved the new shelf space that the stores were offering. But the competitor's sales rep assumed the new decision process would be consistent with the way decisions had always been made in the past. In the past, the category manager would pilot the plan in several stores across the country and see which pilot provided the greatest return. But in this case, the category manager was familiar enough with both products and the marketing strategy from both companies. So he merely did a phone survey of a selected group of stores and made his decision based on the feedback from local store managers. Fortunately Peter had found out about this approach ahead of time, so he was able to contact several of the stores prior to the category manager conducting his survey. Conducting his own research allowed Peter to tailor his approach to better suit his customer's needs, and he developed a smarter strategy to help local store managers see the value in his product. He won this business because he didn't assume the decision process was going to be the same as before.

Where's the Fire? Finding or Creating a Sense of Urgency

One of us loves the thrill of riding roller coasters, such as King's Dominion's Intimidator, named for NASCAR's Dale Earnhardt. Featuring a 300-foot, 85-degree drop and speeds at over 90 mph, the ride lives up to its name. Once the coaster crests the hill, there is almost no stopping it, and we find ourselves looking for our stomachs by the end of the ride.

There are some sales opportunities that remind us of roller coasters. As one of our clients told us, "Sometimes we're lucky and the sense of urgency driving the decision is internal, and all you have to do is hang on and work to influence the decision in your favor." Just like a roller coaster. For other opportunities, we have to create the sense of urgency. As one executive told us, "If there's no burning platform, we have to light one on fire."

Some questions that will help you determine your customer's sense of urgency include:

- What's driving your customer's decision to act?
- Is there a driving force in the market forcing them to act now?
- Does each influencer have the same sense of urgency?

It would be great if your opportunity was the only one on the customer's radar. Unfortunately, that's only true in our sales fantasies. Many other projects are competing for the attention, to say nothing of the time and money, of our customers. Moreover, we are not the only ones buzzing in our customers' ears. Sometimes, these decisions represent a zero-sum game: when one wins approval, other solutions or other projects altogether are immediately put on the back burner. Part of our challenge is keeping the customer's focus on us and convincing them that our product is important to their success.

While working with a major medical device manufacturer that sells bedside monitors, we had the great pleasure of working with Wendy. She was a young, solid performer for her company, attaining the President's Club Award twice in her three-year tenure. Wendy was working with a hospital in the Southwest to replace 300 monitors located in all of the hospital's ICUs. Wendy was fortunate to get her products approved for trial, and the trial process was a success. She thought she had the sale in the bag. However, weeks went by, and she struggled to get access to her contacts within the hospital. After three weeks passed, Wendy finally spoke to her contact. She learned that the plan to replace the monitors was on hold. Wendy was confused. How could the committee put the project on hold after putting forth all the effort to evaluate the replacements? Wendy soon learned that the hospital had just hired a new CFO, someone who had a reputation for scrutinizing spending decisions.

So, what can she do now? Wait until they felt ready to reengage? Wendy was a highly-motivated top performer and driver, and she knew she had to find a way to create a sense of urgency to get the hospital to take action. She knew that the hospital staff preferred her monitor over the competition. But if she didn't light a fire somewhere, the competitor would win by default.

Wendy decided to schedule a meeting with the new CFO, using her advocate to arrange an introduction. Wendy listened to his plans and objectives related to profitability. She demonstrated how her company's track record aligned with the CFO's objectives, specifically demonstrating the link between her product's key strengths and those aims. She found the hospital's sense of urgency, and the deal was back on track. Within the month, her customer had ordered 275 new monitors.

Who's Who in the Zoo: Identifying the Influencers

Both of us like to watch football when it's in season, which it always is, thanks to ESPN, TiVO, and various start-up leagues that compete for our springtime attention. We are drawn to the drama of violent hits and artful grace in well-played contests. But we especially enjoy watching trick plays unfold. One of our favorites is a play called the "fake substitution" or "hideout" play. It relies on equal parts misdirection, confusion, and complacency; not unlike a good magic trick. Most of us who watch football are accustomed to situational substitutions. A linebacker leaves so the defense can bring on an additional defensive back when the situation calls for a pass, or a tight end will be replaced by an additional wideout. It's so common we almost do not notice it, which is why this trick play sometimes works. Just before the snap, a player—usually a receiver or running back—jogs lazily toward his sideline, as though he is being replaced—except that he is not really leaving. At the snap of the ball, he is at the sideline, ready to run upfield and catch the gently-lofted pass, with nothing between him and the end zone. Unfortunately, the play may draw an unsportsmanlike conduct penalty if done incorrectly, but that is a matter for the referees. For us, it's just plain fun.

This play reminds us of one of the cardinal rules in strategic opportunity planning: Know who all the players are at all times. We have all been victims of a "trick play"—we lose a deal because someone behind the scenes preferred our competition. When this happens we may make excuses for ourselves or cry foul. But the truth of the matter is that we just did not notice them. They were right there, standing on the sidelines.

Top performers work very hard at identifying all the potential influencers, both those for us and those against us. What are their roles? How much influence do they have? We will spend a substantial amount of time discussing these questions in the next chapter. For now, when you are assessing the factors underlying a buying decision, it's just about headcount: Who are the influencers and what role do they play?

Robert was a key account executive for a publishing company and the point man for an account team selling to a major grocery retailer. The grocery store was redesigning its customer checkout stations, and Robert and his team were hoping to get new racks placed at all of them. As they discussed their opportunity strategy, one member pointed out that they were overlooking three critical influencers. Apparently two people Robert hadn't even considered were members of a special committee. This special committee was formed by corporate and included managers at the store level. Because Robert doesn't sell at that level, he hadn't considered their role in the grocery store's decision process. Fortunately, he was able to change his strategy to address the store managers' concerns, which were centered around installing checkout racks that didn't block the view of other merchandise. Because Robert's team knew who all the key influencers were in the decision process, his team won the business.

All For One—Solution: Building Consensus Among Influencers

Being able to identify the key influencers involved in a buying decision is obviously critical. However, merely knowing "who's who in the zoo" isn't enough. Another critical best practice is building consensus of opinion around a decision. Building consensus requires being able to answer two key questions.

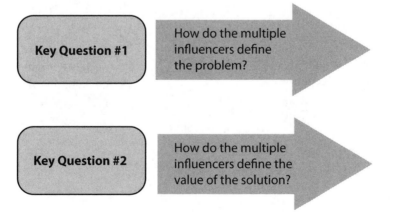

Key Question #1 — How do the multiple influencers define the problem?

Key Question #2 — How do the multiple influencers define the value of the solution?

First, you must have clarity regarding how the multiple buyers define the problem. Second, you need clarity about how the multiple buyers define value in the solution. In Robert's case, if the corporate buyers didn't agree with the challenges of the store managers, the decision could have been delayed or the plan to change the design of the check-out stations totally scrapped. Fortunately for Robert and his team, the corporate buyers and the store managers both had a common understanding of the problem and the desire to fix it.

However, mere consensus on the problem is not enough. Top performers realize that they must connect how the customer defines the problem and the way their product solves it. When a decision includes multiple decision makers, this connection may be complicated and challenging. But failing to make it may result in touchdowns for the opposing team.

Mulitple Influencers in the Decision

The Unique Value of Your Solution

The Usual Suspects? Know the Competition and Their Strengths

Books on strategy extol the virtues of knowing your competition or your enemy. From *The Art of War* to *The Book of Five Rings* to more contemporary volumes, the advice has now passed into commonplace. Know your competition. Do not underestimate them. Undercut their strengths and exploit their weaknesses. It's become fairly vanilla. And while we have nothing against Sun Tzu or Clausewitz or even the *Harvard Business Review*, we prefer to extract lessons on strategizing from pop culture.

Consider *The Usual Suspects*, a film from 1995 with a clever and twisted moral. Kevin Spacey plays Roger "Verbal" Kint, a small-time crook who is one of only two survivors of a massacre at the Port of Los Angeles, who is being interrogated by U.S. Customs agent Dave Kujan, played by Chazz Palminteri. The story, brilliantly and compellingly told, reminds us of some commonplace lessons in selling:

- Expect the unexpected.
- Don't overlook the obvious.
- Never underestimate the enemy.
- Be wary of your own assumptions.

A few years ago we were working with a major printing and publishing company that was competing for a significant new business opportunity.

Tom was a successful account manager for our client and had owned the customer relationship for more than five years. The customer was worth about $4 million annually to Tom's company, which was about 30 percent of the total market share available. Tom's customer wanted to centralize much of the print purchasing to achieve economies of scale and better quality control, but they were struggling to get regional offices to comply.

The regional offices preferred to use local providers for a diverse range of reasons. They were extremely loyal to their local providers, with many of them having community and personal ties. It didn't take a detective to realize that capturing demand from these local providers would be very tough indeed. Moreover, Tom's customer was reluctant to play the heavy. A winning strategy would have to provide a win-win approach.

Instead of positioning himself as their competition, Tom worked to be an ally with the local providers. He could offer regional offices the best of both worlds, which meant that they could use the local providers for the jobs in which they excelled, and use Tom's company for the jobs in which he excelled. This "alliance" approach allowed regional offices to maintain their local connections while at the same time satisfy the corporate mandate to use Tom's company. Tom's success was the result of identifying who his competition was and then formulating a strategy based on their strengths and weaknesses.

Chapter 2 Summary

In this chapter, we covered the key components of understanding your customers' critical buying factors. First, you need to know the length of the decision process. Will this be a marathon or will it be a sprint? Do you need to quickly marshal your resources for a blitzkrieg? Or do you need to keep your powder dry for a long assault? (And please pardon the military metaphors.) The second component you need to understand is whether this particular decision will be made in the same way as previous ones. Is there a guarantee of consistency? Knowing this will help you adjust your approach, the way our friend Peter adapted his in order to sell to his grocery store customer. The third component we've talked about is finding—or creating—a sense of urgency. Why does your customer want to do this? What is driving their decision and how can you keep this burning platform on fire? Next, identify the influencers who will play a role in the customer's decision process. Finally, the fifth component is knowing who the competition is (or are). These comprise both external competitors (your usual suspects, but keeping an eye out for emerging players) and internal competitors (every project competes with other projects for funding and attention—how does yours rank?).

Although we have presented these five factors in a sequence, it would probably be false to say they must be addressed in sequence or in isolation. While there is some utility in categorizing them, looking at them in isolation would be like looking at the world through a straw. The reality is that they are interrelated. What we have seen top performers do is consider each set of factors independently, but with a careful eye at how they interrelate with one another. An opportunity with a short decision cycle, a high sense of urgency, and multiple decision makers unfolds quite a bit differently than one with a long cycle, lower sense of urgency, and fewer decision makers.

Chapter 3
Managing Key Players

It would be tempting to begin this chapter with a quote from Sun Tzu about knowing the enemy and knowing yourself. That quote, while being predictable and almost trite given its frequency of use, is very valuable when it comes to military strategy. But when discussing key players, we are not talking about the opposition or our enemies. We are speaking of our customers. We want to win their favor, not defeat them. So we think military metaphors, while having their place in sales strategizing, should not be in a chapter about knowing who our customers are.

Rather, this chapter on managing the key players in your targeted accounts will draw on another metaphor: that of a successful courtship. For just as the enthusiastic suitor invests time, creativity, effort, and money in knowing his intended beloved, so too do successful sellers invest in their customers. We want to know their ups and downs, their ins and outs. We want to know who they are, what they want, and why they want it. Knowing the key players in your strategically important accounts is one of the most crucial and challenging tasks you will have in the world of complex sales. This chapter, while not providing a magic bullet to make it easy or always successful, will nevertheless give you useful tools and proven best practices to make it manageable.

Harry: The Story of a Bona Fide Suitor

Harry is a sales rep for a corporate wellness solution provider. We were asked to help him in the creation of a strategy for a new opportunity. Once we'd heard the details about the prospect, we first asked Harry to tell us about the key players inside his prospect's organization, the ones who would be responsible for making the decision.

According to Harry, there was a supporter inside the account. It was the individual with whom Harry had spent the most time and who seemed to be helping Harry in the development of a sales strategy. He seemed to love Harry's solution, and Harry clearly hoped to use him as his internal champion. However, his "champion" lacked decision-making authority, and Harry worried that this would hinder his ability to achieve his sales goals. There were others of whom Harry spoke, including one individual Harry viewed as the most troublesome, someone who seemed to be working against him. This person was most definitely not a supporter of Harry's organization and in fact had been known to make negative remarks about Harry's company. And then of course, Harry talked about the "Dude"—the one key individual with whom final authority rested. Unfortunately Harry had no relationship at this level, and his champion had advised against going directly to him. He had recommended instead that Harry work through him. It was a bleak picture, but Harry felt hopeful that his internal champion could help him.

Our next question—"Is there anyone else?"—drew a troubling response: "Um, I don't think so."

Why This Step Matters

Complex sales are *complex*. Avoid the temptation to dismiss this point simply because it states the obvious. The complexity we speak of here relates to the number of people who play roles in major purchasing decisions. There is seldom one Big Kahuna who unilaterally owns the decision. Success in complex selling means managing many different players, a trend that will only increase in worsening economic conditions. Why? The answer might be as simple as the ability to share blame. As companies put greater scrutiny on major purchases, very few want to stand alone on risky decisions. Consensus not only means vetting ideas through more brains; it also means that blame can be spread around.

Don't most salespeople know this already? Certainly, most sellers acknowledge that they are selling to groups today more than they were a decade ago. Our friend Harry's situation wasn't unique, and Harry knew it.

Given that everyone will acknowledge the role of multiple individuals in any buying process, you'd think it would be commonplace for people to have a strategy for managing them. Indeed, most salespeople will tell you that they do have a strategy of sorts. Our friend Harry had one. May we share it?

Harry's strategy was to continue to work with his champion to advance his sales efforts. He hoped his champion would promote his solution to the other key players in the organization, including the highly influential "Dude." Harry wanted the chance to come in and present to others in person, and felt that his champion's efforts might pave the way to a meeting.

Harry also acknowledged the need to proactively address his "enemy"— the individual who seemed to have it out for him and his company— and he had a couple ideas how. One approach was to use his champion to directly confront the enemy, to use his friend to build credibility for his company and solutions. A second, albeit far less serious option, was a dark alley confrontation. Harry's plan, when he thought it through, did not fill him with confidence. In reality, it showed that he really lacked a plan. Why?

Harry, like many other sellers, liked to rely on people he was comfortable with. He preferred to focus his efforts on "friends" rather than "enemies." If his friends were more influential than his enemies, he tended to win. If not, he tended to lose. Given that he typically had more friends than enemies, he usually won more than he lost. The downside, of course, was that he might lose some he should win.

Another reason Harry's plan was lacking has to do with human nature. Most people tend to avoid confrontations. Harry was no different. Calling directly on his enemy was almost unthinkable for Harry. Why would he? It might result in a disagreement, which would certainly be counterproductive. Better to let his friend do his fighting for him in this case. Most salespeople prefer to let champions carry their banner for them, having no real strategy for counteracting or neutralizing apparent enemies such as Harry's.

Selling only inside our "comfort zones" has other downsides, the most prominent of which is that our perspective on the situation tends to be skewed. We only hear one side of the story, and it may be woefully inadequate. Another downside is that our champions may be less influential than we realize. It's not that they can't help us at all, but it may be that they cannot help us enough. So, we ought not to put all of our eggs into one basket, like Harry was attempting to do.

Back to the Drawing Board

Let's go back to the first question we asked Harry: "Who will be involved in the decision?" The second step in developing your sales strategy is to make sure you have thorough knowledge of who will play a role in the decision.

Bob Ross is a famous painter, art instructor, and television host. People of a certain age, including us, remember him for the television show *The Joy of Painting*, which ran for 12 years on PBS. Ross joyfully painted scenic landscapes, usually filled with "happy little trees." Apart from his own personal charm, what made the show interesting was the way he created the painting. Beginning with the background, which he thoroughly painted, he added layer upon layer, moving toward the foreground. And just when you thought he was done, he added another layer, which made the painting richer and more detailed. Building a sales strategy is much like Bob Ross and his paintings. The "picture" you will create is the graphical and narrative depiction of how your customer is going to make his decision. Having it in hand will allow you to determine an appropriate strategy for moving forward.

Beginning with the background, you add layer upon layer until you have a clear and detailed picture. And key players are part of that background. Who should be included? Obviously, not every player is a key player, because not everyone inside your customer's organization is involved in every decision. Each situation is different, so each picture will be different. Those who need to be included in your picture are those who are involved in and have influence over a decision. This could be anyone, frankly, and depends upon many factors that change from sale to sale. But it usually includes people

- who have buying influence
- who will be affected by the decision
- who are influential over others.

It's been our experience that not all key players will be recognizable as such, nor will you necessarily know them by name or title. Top performers tend to cast a wide net at the beginning because they do not want to be blindsided by the surprise entrance of someone they neglected.

Your Preliminary Sketch

Many people feel that there are a number of diverse factors that dictate how important one person is to one decision, such as title, purchasing history, or political sway. But in practice, there are really two factors that ultimately matter—the person's level of influence in this particular decision, and how that individual feels about you and your competition's solution. To help provide a clear picture of the key players in your sales opportunities, let's look at a simple three-step process.

Step 1—Who Is Involved? First, identify all individuals who may potentially play a role. Consider not only those you know by name, but also functional areas. For example, if you do not personally know anyone in procurement but are certain someone will be involved, list procurement. Along with the customer's internal staff, consider whether external resources might be involved, such as consultants or partners. Try not to eliminate any key players out of hand.

Step 2—How Do They Feel? The second step is to consider how each of these players feels about us and our solution, especially when compared to our competition. What is their temperature? Are they for us? Against us? Somewhere in between? We use the following scale:

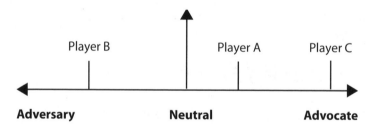

Advocates are our friends, those we would expect to be in our corner in a fight. Ask yourself: Does this person have a preference for us over our competitors? Is he a raving fan (tough to find, by the way, and not always a good thing)? Adversaries, on the other hand, are standing in our way. They are not necessarily in the opposite corner; in fact, they may be trying to shut the fight down altogether. These are the people who want to see us lose, and they may also want to see the other guys lose, too. Is she someone who's spoken openly against us? Is he a raving fan of the competition? Does he have a project or budget that would be hindered by our progress? And what about those who are difficult to measure? Are there some "Switzerlands" in your customer's key player mix, folks who just don't want to take sides?

Step 3—Are They Influential? The third step is to estimate each key player's influence over the decision. How powerful is each of the players? Is he "the" decision maker? He may not be the one who says "yes," but does he have the power to veto a decision? Is she an opinion leader within the organization? Is she known for persuasive skills? These are the sorts of questions you should ask. We can use a similar scale to map a key player's influence.

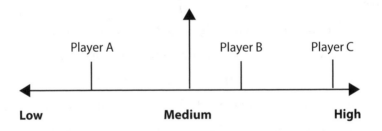

The measure of someone's influence is typically very specific to the opportunity at hand. His influence may wax or wane, depending on many factors, including but not limited to his title and function. Someone who is highly influential may have the final "yes" authority. On the other hand, he may be the one with the power to rain all over your burning platform.

Picking Up Your Brush: The Key Player Map

To assemble a "Key Player Map," combine these two simple scales, as shown in the figure on the following page. When you complete the map, you will often find a "picture" that is unique to the situation in which you are working. Decisions are not always made in the same fashion, even inside the same organization. It is important to remember that this picture will be unique for almost every decision, with different players having varying levels of influence and varying "temperatures" about the potential suppliers.

Creating your sketch of the key players seems simple, doesn't it? Yet appearances can be deceiving. Like Bob Ross and his famous paintings, just when you think it's done, it's not. Populating the map is a simple task. But that doesn't mean it's easy. Even at its best, the process involves some guesswork about where folks lie along the spectrums. Effective sales strategies work thoroughly to build the framework, but do not set it in stone. Too much can change over the long course of a complex sale. Moreover, assumptions may very well turn out to be wrong. With apologies to the band 38 Special, "Hold on loosely, but don't let go."

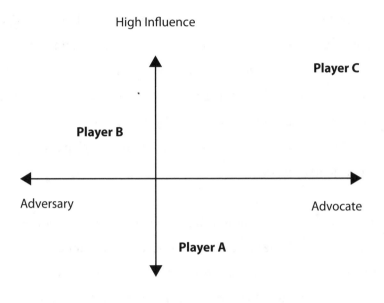

High Influence

Player C

Player B

Adversary   Advocate

Player A

Low Influence

Knowing how things stand with key players is always advantageous, if not always comforting. But even if this mapping process reveals how poor your situation is, it at least allows you to understand where you are.

We put this concept to work with our friend Harry. In order to get a more complete picture of the decision makers and influencers, we asked Harry to broaden his evaluation of key players inside his prospective account. We even included Harry's advocate in the discussion, mostly because Harry lacked real understanding of who might actually influence the decision.

The picture of the key players looked a lot different after the discussion. In fact, there were seven people (up from the original three) who would have some influence over the decision to implement Harry's solution. The unfortunate thing is that Harry's relative position wasn't any better. In fact it was worse. But by having gained a better understanding of where he stood, Harry could now develop a strategy that might actually work.

There are two main goals in going through the mapping process. First, the process can give you a reasonably clear and accurate picture of the key players and their importance in the decision. It is a quick visual not just of who's who in the zoo, but which of them ought to be let out of their cages. The second goal of the process is to help create a strategy for improving your true position. Sometimes the map does not reveal what you know as much it reveals what you don't know. This too is helpful. There may be key players you are unable to map because you do not know either how influential they are or how they feel about you. These gaps can help establish your next steps.

Research, as well as practical experience, tells us that many minds considering a problem will yield better solutions. This is especially true in developing sales strategies. Left to our own devices, we tend to rely on our assumptions. We are too close to the situation to be genuinely creative or insightful. Bringing others into the mix will shake things up, introduce fresh perspective, and yield unexpected and powerful insights. Having a simple visual representation of your stance will allow you to bring others up to speed quickly. They can challenge your thinking, poke holes in your assumptions, and raise new questions about your approach. In the end, your picture will be richer and more complete.

You've Drawn the Picture; Now What?

Research on sales planning is pretty clear: There is not a significant amount of difference between average and successful performers when it comes to the time spent developing a strategy. Average performers and top performers tend to spend about the same amount of time on it. What is different is *how* they spend their time. Average performers tend to emphasize gathering information, while top performers tend to emphasize what to do with it. Put another way, average performers spend the majority of their time figuring out what they want, while top performers spend the majority of their time figuring out how they are going to get what they want. In simplest terms, you might say this is the difference between preparation and planning.

Putting the map together is preparation. *Doing* something with the information is planning. What does successful planning look like? Consider the following ideas.

Strengthening Your Position

Certainly the greatest objective when looking at your Key Player Map is to determine ways to tip the scale in your favor, and that means figuring out how to create more influential advocates. That being said, every picture, regardless of where people stand on the grid, should encourage you to develop a strategy to improve your situation or preserve it.

Utilizing Your Advocates

Your greatest asset is a strongly influential advocate. These champions can help you develop a strategy for improving your picture and planning your next steps. You can also use them to counteract your adversaries. Their influence makes them extremely important.

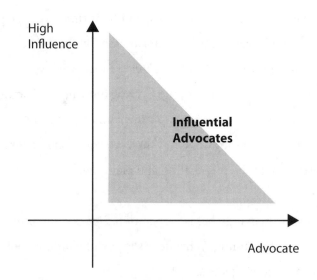

However, having influential advocates has at least two traps lying in wait. Our friend Harry fell into the trap of over-relying on his advocate to champion his solution. He had hoped for the best, but as the wise man said, "Wishful thinking is not exactly a strategy." The second trap ready to be sprung is over-focusing on the others in the organization because your advocate is already sold. You may think, "Why bother preaching to the choir? She's already in our camp." This often leaves your strongest champion open for the competition to sway her, which makes for a very nasty surprise come decision day.

Even if your greatest asset is your influential advocates does not mean you can ignore everyone else. On the contrary, it might be useful to pay even closer attention to them as you develop your plan. What do you do with the influencer who opposes you? Can they be turned? What about the advocate who has little influence? Are there ways you can help them gain stature in the organization, thereby increasing their influence? It would be unusual to have someone whose influence cannot be increased. This is because influence on a decision is not typically positional (that is, title is not equivalent to level of influence). Helping your less influential advocates understand the scope of the problem you are solving and its impact on the company, as well as quantifying the payoff of your proposed solution, can be crucial in their gaining more influence. Do they understand the "pain and the gain"? Can they effectively communicate them to other decision influencers?

Also, how certain are you of your advocates' influence or their loyalty to you? Is there a risk that they may feel the same enthusiasm for your competitor's solution? Are they willing to "sell" your ideas to others?

Once you have become absolutely certain that an individual is your advocate and yours alone, then the question becomes, "What will they do to help you, by influencing others in the organization who are adversaries or as yet undecided?"

In Harry's case, his champion was truly his advocate. This individual had worked with Harry's company and knew the power of their solutions. He had also been championing Harry's company before the real opportunity actually presented itself. And lastly, this person had proven to be supportive of Harry by arranging meetings and speaking to others on Harry's behalf. Harry now had to find additional ways to leverage his advocate's support.

Creating Advocates

More selling happens at your customer's site when you are not there than when you are. So, your advocates' support is crucial. How do we find advocates? They do not just drop from the sky, but they do grow on trees. Sort of. Salespeople have to plant and then nourish them carefully, like they would a valuable plant. Here are some suggestions that have paid dividends:

1. Present solutions that help them succeed in their jobs.

2. Strive to be an asset which they can use to improve their image.

3. Be a value-added resource who isn't always trying to sell them something, but rather who is trying to help them in as many ways possible.

4. Don't "love 'em and leave 'em"; keep in constant contact with them to continually build the relationship.

5. Ask them for help (after you've earned the right).

6. Use other champions to help you determine who else is likely to be a helpful advocate—someone who has authority and respect within their organization (it isn't going to be all that helpful to have a key advocate that no one likes, respects, or listens to).

Dealing With Adversaries

Whenever we help a sales team draw a Key Player Map and then ask them what they are going to do about their adversaries, the responses are often comical. First there is silence, followed by the proposal of a diabolical plot to have the person's kneecaps broken in the parking lot! We know these answers are in jest (or at least we hope so), but the first genuine reaction from almost everyone is befuddled confusion. Fortunately, there are approaches which experience has shown to be useful in counteracting and managing adversaries.

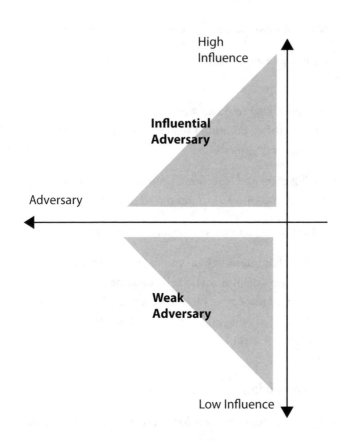

First, you need to know why they are against you. Is it that they truly dislike you, your company, or your products? Or are they just more favorable toward a competitor? It is important to figure out if they are actively hostile toward you, or simply in favor of your competitor.

We tend to view all adversaries as bad news, but some news is worse than others. The actively hostile adversary is, in some ways, much more dangerous than the passively opposed. On the other hand, we have seen actively hostile adversaries overplay their position and compromise their influence. And while passively opposed adversaries may not be as uncomfortable to us (we tend to attribute their opposition to simple ignorance), they are also often tough to persuade.

There is no one-size-fits-all approach to dealing with adversaries. Your strategies and tactics have to take into account many factors, among them the adversaries' levels of influence and their degree of hostility.

In our friend Harry's case, there were two types of adversaries, and they required different types of approaches. The first adversary was someone who presented a significant roadblock. In fact, Harry called her a "roadside bomb." She had been responsible for bringing in the existing wellness program, and viewed any additional programs as a threat to her own. She knew very little about Harry's company or its capabilities, but had still managed to plant significant doubt over Harry's solutions among the decision team. So on the one hand, she was an assailant and creating an impact that Harry couldn't ignore. On the other hand, she did not seem to have an extraordinary level of influence, even though she was making a lot of noise.

The second adversary in Harry's situation was, interestingly enough, more powerful than the first. She was a skeptic of Harry's solutions, but didn't have any allegiance to Harry's competitors. She was highly influential, but only moderately adversarial. Harry felt she would be easier to deal with, and that there was a chance to change this person from adversary to advocate with the right approach.

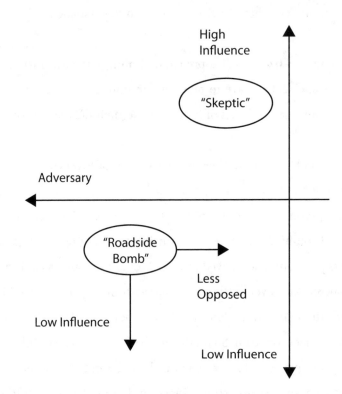

Regardless of why someone is an adversary, the goal is to make this person either less opposed to you or less influential in the decision-making process. The challenge is in making that happen. This is why a complete assessment of the key players within a buying opportunity is critical. Your key player picture is what helps you determine the best course of action.

Don't Forget the Neutrals

The trap embedded in your neutral territory is to spend too much time working with advocates or minimizing the damage of adversaries, while ignoring the folks in the middle. The advocates and adversaries have to come from somewhere—usually from the neutral middle. If you don't try to convert a "neutral" into an advocate, your competition will, and then this previously passive player becomes your new adversary.

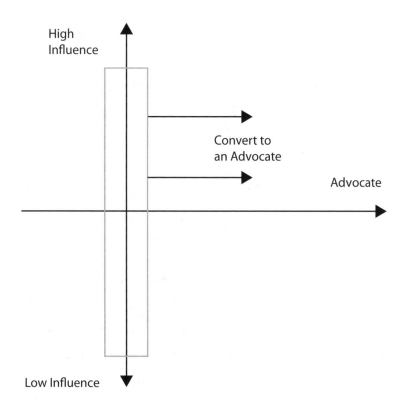

Courting Your Customer

One of our favorite films is Harold Ramis's brilliant comedy *Groundhog Day*, starring Bill Murray. The story is about a Pittsburgh weatherman named Phil Connors (Murray's character) who is compelled to repeat the same day—Groundhog Day—over and over again. A beautifully sweet fable with profound underlying themes about selfishness, self-lessness, and the meaning of life, it also paints a pretty good metaphor for complex selling.

Phil, who has fallen in love with Rita, his producer, begins spending all of his Groundhog Days learning everything he can about her. He learns her history, her likes and dislikes, her preferences and tastes, her dreams. It gets to the point where they finally have this exchange (after countless repeated days in which he learns more and more about her):

Rita: This day was perfect. You couldn't have planned a day like this.

Phil: Well, you can. It just takes an awful lot of work.

Getting to know your key players is a lot like Phil Connors' efforts with Rita. Who are they? What do they want? Why do they want it? You do not have to be omniscient or omnipotent. You just have to invest the time. As Phil tells Rita, speaking of God: "Maybe he's not omnipotent. Maybe he's just been around so long he knows everything."

Chapter 3 Summary

In this chapter, we explained the steps to managing key players in your accounts. The first step is to identify all the key players who might play a role in the decision. The list should include players you personally know and players you may not personally know. Next, determine whether each key player is an advocate or an adversary. What is their temperature toward your solution? Do you they like you or not? The third step is to gauge their influence, which may vary according to the sort of decision that is being considered.

As you add layers to your picture by populating the Key Player Map, it is important not to hold too tightly to your original sketch, as the players' positions may change over time. Someone who is cool today may warm up to you over time. Someone who lacks influence now may become more influential.

After the picture is formed and your potential vulnerabilities emerge, it is crucial to begin strengthening your position. Emphasize your strengths, minimize your weaknesses. In particular, this means developing influential advocates and overcoming influential adversaries, while not neglecting those who appear neutral.

Chapter 4

Knowing Your Environment

Almost every culture has stories that tell of adventurers traversing wild and untamed lands on glorious quests. It seems that in all of mankind there dwells a latent spirit of adventure, which occasionally rises to the forefront. J.R.R. Tolkien's masterpiece, *The Hobbit,* is one such example. Tolkien drew on more classical examples, from *The Odyssey* to tales of St. Brendan the Navigator. These stories have as a common component the idea of "circumstantial uncertainty," a phrase used by the American writer Mark Batterson (2008) to describe adventure's underlying foundation: the uncertainty and unpredictability of life, full of seemingly random and unexpected occurrences that alter our thinking and change our course.

Selling in today's economy exemplifies this truth, perhaps more now than at any time in our past. One day, you are working a major deal with a heavy-hitting prospect; the next, your main advocate is looking for work and you are scrambling to refill your pipeline.

Change, they say, is the only constant. We have heard that mantra for more than two decades now, so much so that its familiarity has robbed it of its power. But it is nevertheless true: We live and work in a world of circumstantial uncertainty, and sometimes the winds blow fair, sometimes they blow foul. One guarantee is that the business environment we sell in today will not be the same the next morning.

Riding Out Storms

One of us is an avid boater. Some time ago, we participated in an annual Poker Run sponsored by a local marina. The rules of each Poker Run are relatively straightforward and simple. The captain and his crew take their boat to five different stops along the course (in this case, the Potomac River) and pick up playing cards. At the final destination, each crew plays their best hand.

Prior to going out that day, weather forecasters warned of the possibility of late afternoon thunderstorms, a common occurrence in the summer where we live. So, before pushing away from the docks that day, we made certain we had everything necessary for a safe and fun day on the river. Our GPS and VHF radio were in good working order. We had plenty of fuel. Our life jackets were ready if we needed them. And we had plenty of food and beverages (beyond having enough grog for the crew, of course).

We pushed off mid-morning, and true to expectations, we were having a grand time on the river (and we were soon working on a royal flush, but that is another story). The weather had cleared up nicely by noon, and we naturally concluded that the weather forecasters were in error. (Some day, we will tackle the subject of sales forecasting and use meteorologists as our working model for how *not* to do it, but that is for another book.) By the early afternoon, however, the lovely and clear blue skies of the morning had begun to take on a threatening haze. By late afternoon ominous dark clouds crowded overhead, while the wind had begun to kick up spray and chop. Our fun little Poker Run had taken a nasty turn.

Wanting to put safety first, the event's coordinator cut things short and advised all crews to head back to the marina. The entire regatta of 50 boats began to head north on the Potomac toward the marina and safe havens. Unfortunately for most of us, this did not mean we escaped the encroaching weather. Within 20 minutes, our boat was fighting its way through six-foot waves coming over our bow, a steady torrent of rain, and wind gusts that felt like mini tornadoes. With life jackets belted firmly on, everyone on the crew began to batten down hatches to keep the boat from taking on water. Our environment had changed in an instant, though we were bravely slogging through with stiff upper lips. We did not count, however, on our engine being swamped and stalling. Not 30 minutes after the weather had turned foul, we were a big fiberglass cork being tossed around by an angry Mother Nature, completely at the mercy of the river. Waves were still slamming the boat and all we could do was try to keep our bow facing into the wind, an effort that was practically futile without power. Praying was at the forefront of some agendas. And of course, we called for help on our thankfully functional VHF radio. We gave them the GPS coordinates and waited for help.

Happily for us, another captain saw that we were in distress and came alongside to provide us support. He tied our boats together and stuck with us until the Coast Guard arrived. Forty-five minutes after it started, our summer squall had passed, its damage done: a lost engine, and one crewmember's lunch (literally—he had set it by the rail and it was washed overboard). The Coast Guard towed us home and we were none the worse for wear, thankful that it was not more serious.

How many of us have had client engagements that we would compare to boating in the midst of a storm, when you are being kicked around by the environment and losing control of things? Every salesperson, from the average to the top performer, runs into things they do not expect—and could not have predicted—during the long and winding journey of a complex sales cycle. Unanticipated circumstances, like a summer storm, can arise with very little warning. What makes the difference between simply surviving and thriving is not necessarily the accuracy of your predictions, but rather your level of preparedness and your ability to adapt to the changing environment.

Think about a typical sales opportunity for a moment. What are some of the critical events that could affect your winning it? There are events that could positively and negatively influence the opportunity. A few that come to mind may be:

- Your most strongly influential advocate has left your customer's organization.

- Your competitor's product has been recalled, leaving the field clear for you.

- A key supporter of your solutions at another company has joined your customer's organization in a position of influence.

- Your company has experienced either product quality or service delivery failures, and the word is spreading in the market.

- Your customer experiences a significant financial downturn (or windfall).

Have you considered these possibilities? What have you done to reduce your risks or strengthen your position? How can you capitalize on positive turns or mitigate the negative ones? We will never be able to predict all eventualities, either positive or negative. However, if we have thought the possibilities through, we will be better prepared to deal with them if they do occur. When we left the docks for our annual Poker Run, we were well prepared for the unexpected. Life jackets, working radio, GPS, food, and water. We did not expect to lose our engine, but we were able to weather that "circumstantial uncertainty" because we had taken other precautions.

Selling in uncertain times means remembering that part of the old Boy Scout oath: "Be prepared."

Preparing for Threats Near and Far: Two Ways of Viewing the Environment

Top performers look at their selling environment in two ways. What could happen nearby—in my company, my customer's company—that could affect our success? We might call this nearby view a micro-view. Looking at things near at hand gives you a limited perspective, however. Top performers also invest time in considering what we call the macro-view. What are those potential events in the world at large that could affect us? How do our customers fit into the bigger picture? How will they be moved by sea changes that can affect an entire industry or market? Top performers are stubbornly pessimistic in their analysis, so they can avoid nasty surprises—or at least are better prepared to deal with them.

The Environment From a Micro-View

A few years ago, we were working with a global medical device manufacturer. This company is the leader in their sector worldwide, with a very solid reputation for outstanding service and great products. Carlos was a top performer at the company. He managed his territory well, he understood his customers' needs, and he delivered on his promises. Not only had he built great relationships with all of his customers, but he also knew who all the key players were in his accounts. He knew his advocates and his adversaries, and knew which ones ranked high and low on the influence scale. Moreover, he was well aware of how things stood with his competitors. He knew their strengths and weaknesses and routinely developed plans to handle any unexpected surprises. In many ways, Carlos was the exemplary major account manager.

One afternoon, Carlos learned that a crucial advocate in one of his hospitals, its director of materials management, was leaving for a new opportunity. Although this was unsettling news, as it would be for anyone who has lost a key supporter, Carlos was confident that his time spent building relationships with other key players inside the hospital was now about to pay dividends. Although the director had been his most influential advocate, she was not the only one.

Carlos, like many others involved with the account, presumed that the director's replacement would be someone promoted from within. The surprise choice, however, was someone from another hospital. Unfortunately for Carlos, the new hire was not a supporter. Everyone was on high alert. Would Carlos and his company be replaced?

Carlos wasn't going to take any chances. His hastily revised strategy involved contacting all his advocates to resell the value of his solution. He prepared executive briefings to remind them of the reasons they initially preferred his solution. He highlighted the differences between his and his competitors' offerings, and helped his key players understand the potential downsides of making a change.

Within four months of being hired, the new director of materials management signaled his intention to displace Carlos and his solution with a lower priced option. Fortunately for Carlos, the new director was open to having conversations with his team—and with the competing vendors—about the intended change. Carlos took this opportunity to find out what the director's selection criteria for the solutions were, and found that price was a primary criterion. The director had developed a financial justification for swapping out Carlos's offering for a lower priced replacement.

The good news for Carlos was that other factors were being considered apart from price. Carlos had invested his time and efforts in cultivating strongly influential advocates who understood the overall value of his solutions. They used their influence to champion Carlos's cause. The change never happened and Carlos continues to grow his market share within that hospital.

Carlos, like all top performers, is a keen observer of his customers' environments. He monitors them carefully and is therefore able to be proactive in his strategies for managing change and uncertainty. He understood there was a chance that a non-supporter of his products could become a key decision maker in his account, so he had to develop a strategy that could defend his position in it. What could have happened if Carlos didn't immediately take steps to lock in his products at the hospital? What if he had waited until the new director of materials management was hired and *then* began developing his sales strategy? Thinking ahead—and putting a strategy together to capitalize on or combat those events that affect the decision-making process—is just smart business.

The Environment From a Macro-View

The butterfly effect is the idea that the flap of a butterfly's wings in Asia has ramifications for the streets of Manhattan. This is at the same time poetic hyperbole and fundamental truth. The events taking place in our world are all interconnected to some degree. And while a single butterfly in a Thai paddy field may not roil the financial markets on Wall Street, we no longer have the luxury of living in a silo. It is vitally important that we look at trends, news, market shifts, and "human factors" that impact our industry sector, as well as other sectors connected to ours. We need to understand how these events are influencing our customers, and more specifically, how they are affecting individuals inside our customers' organizations.

Do you stay on top of the trends in your industry? Do you know what your customers are doing to mitigate risks or capitalize on windfalls? How does this affect you and your company? What are your customers' strategic goals? How do these goals fit within the sector's value chain, from supplier to supplier and to the market? How tight is credit? What effect does access to capital have on your customers, and what bearing does that have on your ability to gain market share with them?

In June 2009, the World Health Organization declared a pandemic. A new virus strain of swine-origin H1N1 was spreading at a rapid rate. By the beginning of 2010, the virus had caused 17,000 deaths. Within six months, hospitals who had been relying on a "just-in-time" approach to procure gloves, masks, gowns, and drapes had shifted to a "just-in-case" stockpiling. With shortages looming, many hospitals operated in near-crisis mode. This trend was wreaking havoc on not only specific suppliers, but also on the entire supply chain.

We were working at that time with an industry-leading supplier that was trying to weather the storm. One of its top performers was Susan. She recognized that this trend was affecting all of her customers in some significant way. A few of her customers had a greater sense of urgency and put higher demands on her. At first, Susan was thrilled with the fact that all of her customers were placing large orders. She couldn't process the purchase orders fast enough. But the fun came to a halt when Susan's company told her that they could not ship products due to a manufacturing backlog. What was Susan going to do? She knew that if she couldn't deliver on those orders, the customers would go to the competition. In the short term, it would mean lost revenue and bad will. But what would be the long term impact? Would this be the beachhead her competitors had long sought? The opportune moment to displace her?

Susan and her colleagues had much to consider as they pondered their options and a strategic, workable response to the crisis. One piece of encouragement came from the fact that the entire sector was likely in similar straits—demand had outstripped supply, and most of Susan's competitors were in no better position to deliver than Susan was. In some areas of the United States, elective surgical procedures were being put on hold because the hospital didn't have the surgical gloves and masks necessary for them. Hospitals had begun to develop proactive strategies to combat this trend.

Working with Susan, we developed an approach we called *ICE,* which stands for Industry, Company, and Executive. It's a simple acronym to remind us of an effective way to assess the buying environment from a macro-view.

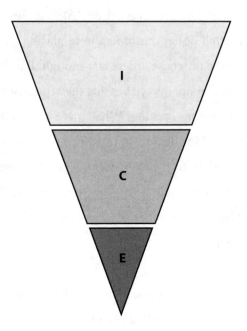

Susan first looked at her industry. What were the trends? Were they long-term or short-term? How were those trends affecting her customers? Her customers' other suppliers? In Susan's case, the shortage of gloves and masks was significantly changing how a hospital operated on a daily basis. Although most people regarded this shortage as a short-term trend, Susan wondered what the long-term ramifications would be. How would this change the way hospitals managed their supply chain?

Susan next narrowed her focus to the company, not only the hospitals in question, but also the competitors against whom Susan was selling. What were they all doing to counteract this market trend—or capitalize on it? Susan observed that some hospitals were making the decision to delay elective surgical procedures. Many were performing only emergency procedures or presently scheduled ones.

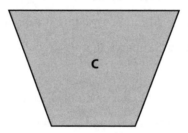

The final part of Susan's ICE strategy focused on the executives inside her customers' companies. What was the effect of the trend on them, and what were their responsibilities? To whom were they accountable?

How were they measured? What goals and objectives did they have, and how were the trends affecting them?

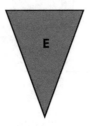

Susan knew that in the height of the crisis, the directors were in reactive modes, simply trying to find inventory to support the needs of their hospitals. A few of the directors were keenly disappointed that Susan's company could not meet their demand. Susan told us that she believed they felt betrayed. They have been loyal customers of hers, and now she was not delivering when they needed her most. Susan knew her position was precarious. After all, loyalty to a supplier is a completely secondary consideration compared to operational readiness.

Susan decided that speaking to her customers' leadership—in most cases, the hospital administrators—would give her a valuable perspective on their plans to deal with widespread shortages. She soon discovered that her top four hospitals had chosen a similar, two-fold approach.

First, they had decided that all inventories of gloves and masks would be controlled solely by the hospitals' Materials Management groups (in other words, their new approach was characterized by centralized purchasing and inventory control). Secondly, each hospital dictated that the type of glove and mask that would be used throughout the hospital would be chosen by Materials Management rather than by clinicians. Clinical staff no longer made the decisions regarding what type of glove or mask could be used in their departments. The goals of these hospitals was to continue to offer safe, high levels of quality care to their communities, even if it meant frustrating the preferences of their medical staffs.

For Susan, this was an extremely disadvantaged course of action given her strong position among the user community. Though the clinical staffs preferred her company's products, during this time of crisis their personal preferences no longer mattered. The hospitals merely distributed whatever gloves and masks they had in inventory to the different departments.

In one of Susan's hospitals, the Materials Management group was distributing two additional manufacturers' gloves and masks because Susan' company couldn't supply enough inventory. What could Susan do to ensure that when the pandemic of the H1N1 virus passed and inventories returned to normal, her customers would want to continue to use her products?

After thoroughly assessing her buying environment, Susan eagerly sought the involvement of her senior management. After all, they had as much at stake in this as she did. They decided to implement a two-part strategy. Part one involved high-level executive contact. Susan and her leadership met with each director of materials management. The purpose of these meetings was to allow the customer to be heard, and to demonstrate how important each one was to Susan's company. Susan also thought it might be a good idea for the customer to have a better understanding of how the pandemic was affecting supply worldwide. The hope was that if both parties shared in the impact of the crisis, then they might jointly be able to come up with new, alternative approaches to navigating the troubled waters.

Part two of the strategy was to meet with each of Susan's key users in her hospital accounts. She planned to talk with them about the crisis and help them understand why she couldn't fulfill their needs. And while the influence of clinicians on purchasing decisions seemed to be waning, she was not certain this was a long-term trend. So she also invested time in reconvincing her advocates that her products were a better match for their hospitals. In other words, she validated the superiority of her product, but emphasized the effect the current crisis was having on her ability to deliver it.

Top performers like Susan understand that to be successful in a hyper-competitive market, they must be proactive. They must pay close attention to the trends in the *industry*, learn how those trends are affecting their *customer*, and learn what goals and new responsibilities the *executives* they sell to must meet. By being prepared and using the tools at their disposal, they can better weather the storms that inevitably surround unexpected events, not just surviving, but perhaps even thriving.

Chapter 4 Summary

Complex selling often involves unexpected turns of events. Just like the weather, it is not completely predictable. This chapter discussed how to prepare for—and in some cases, prevent—the unexpected turn of events. Just as a boat captain prepares for inclement weather by taking proper precautions, the successful salesperson can take steps to put herself in a good position to survive and thrive during "circumstantial uncertainty."

First, it is important to fully understand your environment from both a macro-and micro-perspective. From the micro-perspective, you can thoroughly understand your customer. Who are the advocates and adversaries, as well as the neutrals? What is their level of influence on this decision? What may be changing in that picture? From a macro-perspective, you can understand how your customer is affected by external events. What is happening in its industry? What are the other players doing? Are there far-off events that will have effects on your customer? How? One approach to understanding the environment, and then deciding what to do about it, is something we have dubbed *ICE*. *I* is for *industry*; pay attention to industry trends. *C* is for *company* (customers and competitors). How do the wider industry trends affect both your customer and your competitor? And *E* is for *executive*. What goals and responsibilities do your customer's leading executives have? How can you align with them?

Chapter 5

Influencing the Competitive Landscape

"We aren't looking at any alternatives to your solution. We want to work with you and no one else." Wouldn't it be nice to hear those magical words? While it is possible that some of you reading this chapter have been in the enviable position of facing virtually no competition for a deal, it unfortunately doesn't happen very often. In fact, some would argue that if you have a proper understanding of the term "competition," then the situation of "no competition" does not exist.

What Is Competition?

We were working with Rich, a successful sales representative for a large financial services company. Rich's company specialized in expense management data gathering and analytics via software tools. These tools were created to help companies better analyze employee spending habits and identify areas where savings could be obtained. Rich was working on an opportunity in which he faced serious competition from a large national software company.

Rich's strategy for this opportunity was built around the competitive strengths and weaknesses of this one competitor, with hardly any attention given to other potential competitive threats. When we asked Rich to describe the competitive landscape for this opportunity, this was the first and only competitor he named. When we asked him if there were other alternatives the customer might choose, he responded, "Nothing serious. It's pretty much us or them."

Is competitive analysis and strategy really this simple? A choice between two alternatives?

What Does Webster Say?

Webster's Dictionary offers one definition of competition: "The effort of two or more parties acting independently to secure the business of a third party by offering the most favorable terms."

When we introduce the idea of competitive analysis to our clients, most begin the discussion with *Webster's* definition in mind. They think only of their traditional, familiar competitors, ones who play in the same sandbox and sell similar solutions. This is exactly the framework Rich was using when we asked him to do a competitive analysis. What we find is that most salespeople tend to ignore nontraditional forms of competition. For instance, what about the competition coming from inside our customers' own organizations? In a "make or buy" scenario, this is often where the strongest competitors lie. Because of the way budgets are allotted, internal competition for the same pool of money or resources is completely normal and customary. Choosing your solution is only one alternative among many for the customer. (See the figure on page 75 for a breakdown of the typical alternatives from which a customer can choose.)

Consequently, when we discuss competitive analysis with our clients, the first task before us is to remove their blinders and get them to look beyond the "traditional" competitors. Every alternative before their customer should be considered a legitimate competitor, and a well-thought-out competitive analysis needs to reflect the breadth of choices the customer has before them.

We decided to press Rich in an attempt to stretch his thinking about his competition. The first assumption to test was how limited the competition really was. Was it simply a binary choice? At first, Rich was uncertain, but he did acknowledge that there were some small companies that might go after the business. Rich identified them as boutique consultants and did not feel they were serious competitors. In his opinion, they lacked a track record. Rich also acknowledged that his customer's internal IT department could build a homegrown solution, but he didn't believe that was likely. The company was continually strapped for resources in general and lacked the expertise needed for a project like this in particular. Rich admitted that there were competing priorities inside the company that could feasibly interfere with his project; however, he was confident that his project had priority because it had already been delayed for two years. Rich was sure the company would move forward and felt confident that it was a two-horse race.

Decisions, Decisions: How Does Your Customer Choose?

Competitive analysis isn't complicated, even when there are a large number of competitors in the mix. Customers typically make buying decisions following a reasonably predictable pattern. First, they determine which criteria are important to them in a solution. Second, they look at alternative options and evaluate them against the criteria they determined in step one. And lastly, they select the option that best aligns with their priorities. This is a reasonable approach to decision making, and regardless of how we might perceive them, in this regard prospects are generally reasonable (and predictable).

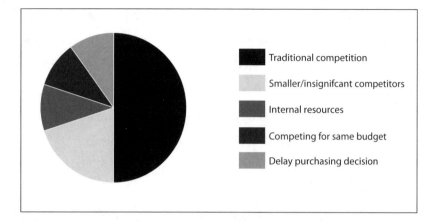

Legend:
- Traditional competition
- Smaller/insignifcant competitors
- Internal resources
- Competing for same budget
- Delay purchasing decision

Selection Criteria

The guidelines by which customers evaluate what's important to them are called *selection criteria*. Let's assume, for example, that you could only choose to enroll in one frequent flyer program. How would you choose the program? What attributes would you consider important? Would you look for a program with more pre-boarding perks, such as an airport lounge or early boarding for members? Or would a program that made it easier to use rewards points be more important to you? Would you like a program with exceptional e-communication capabilities, such as electronic boarding passes or flight status alerts sent to your mobile device? Or would you rather have a program that had a broad partner base, allowing you to use mileage credit for things other than flights? Your customers go through a similar process to determine what's important to them and what is incidental. Our first task is to uncover our customers' selection criteria.

After compiling a list of selection criteria you think your customer may use, it makes sense to consider whether there are any criteria that the customer hasn't even considered, but that they should think about. By creating a more comprehensive list of all possible selection criteria, we enable our customers to make better choices, and we give ourselves the building blocks for a well-thought-out competitive analysis.

Ranking the Criteria

After compiling a comprehensive list of criteria, the next task is to rank order them, from most important to least. Returning to our frequent flyer program example, we might start the process by asking, "What's most important to you in a frequent flyer program?" What are the "must-haves" and what are the "nice-to-haves" on the list? While the questions could be posed in a number of different ways, the desired outcome is insight into how your customer will evaluate the various alternatives from which they could choose.

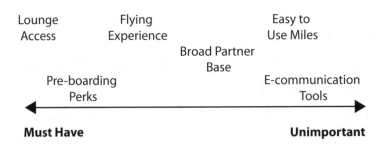

Inevitably, these lists create conflict between competing "desires." To use our frequent flyer example, superior partner programs might be as highly desirable as a network of hospitality lounges. If both are considered highly important, how do you break the tie? So the next question to ask is, "How do you rank criteria relative to each other?" They must have a relative ranking. Even if a customer considers several "crucial" criteria, ultimately they have to choose between them.

For many customers (and for people in general), this is a difficult task. The question here is, "What are you willing to sacrifice?" You can't have the best quality for the cheapest price—at least not usually.

Diane is a sales representative for one of the top cruise lines in the world. Diane's primary customers are travel agents who book cruises on her ships, as well as the ships of her competitors. Because Diane's customers are routinely visited by sales representatives from other cruise lines, Diane's greatest challenge is capturing and retaining what might be called "mind share"—that is, trying to keep herself near the forefront of her customers' minds.

When we first began working with Diane and her company, she was in the midst of competing for an opportunity to book a large corporate sales meeting on one of her ships. A travel agent in her territory had been approached by a company looking to host its annual sales meeting aboard a cruise ship, and the travel agent was trying to determine which cruise line to award the business. The company had asked the travel agent to contact all the major cruise lines to find the best fit for their needs and budget.

Like all top performers we have worked with, Diane had a thorough familiarity with her strengths and weaknesses relative to her competitors. So going in, she knew she would not be the low-cost option. To win, she would have to take the customer's attention off price and emphasize her strengths.

Fortunately, Diane had done her homework. She had learned what the end user's selection criteria looked like. In order of importance, the selection criteria were:

Rank	Selection Criteria	Defined by the Customer
1	Capacity	Able to effectively serve/cater to the dining and meeting needs of the company's entire group (about 200 people) in a single location on the ship
2	Quality	Quality of stateroom accommodations
3	Price	Price per passenger
4	Activities	Ability to specialize both on-board and port-of-call activities for the company's employees
5	Partners	Ability to work special arrangements with air carriers and other travel partners
6	Ship	Age and quality of the ship

Diane had taken an excellent first step in developing a competitive analysis, which would ultimately provide insights into what needed to happen next.

How Do You Measure Up?

Discovering and ranking selection criteria is the first step in the competitive analysis process. The next step is to understand competitive advantages and disadvantages. Like doing a competitive Strengths, Weaknesses, Opportunities, and Threats (SWOT) analysis, this requires gaining insight into how the customer evaluates the options available. In Diane's case, this meant assessing both the travel agent's and the end-user's perspectives of her ship. Did they match up with Diane's own perspective on her areas of strength and weakness?

May we share a personal story? Years ago, Kevin and his wife were considering relocation from their home in the Washington, DC area. When they were evaluating their geographic options, one of their major selection criteria was weather. Kevin says, "My wife does not like heat and humidity, which ruled out portions of the Southeast and Southwest. And I didn't like places that experienced snowfalls any later than February, which eliminated much of the Northeast and parts of the central plains. So, out of our short list of cities, we selected Portland, Oregon, which is very well known for having abundant cloud coverage and lots of rain." When he explains to people how they made their decision, and mentions that Portland had a relative position of strength with regard to weather, people look at him with surprise. Portland wins with weather? It's all in how you define it.

Analysis of strengths reminds us of the proverbs: "Beauty is in the eye of the beholder" or, "One person's trash is another person's treasure." A salesperson might firmly believe he is strong with regard to a specific criterion, but his opinion matters little. It's what the customer believes that is important. We have to look at the selection criteria through the customer's eyes. Doing this will reveal what we must do to improve our competitive position.

Customer's Perception of Us Versus Competing Alternatives

| Strong | Comparable | Weak |

Getting your customer to describe honestly how you stack up to their selection criteria can be challenging for a couple reasons. First, some customers may be reluctant to be truthful because they do not want to risk offending you. A second reason may be that they do not want to give you any negotiating leverage. A third reason can be that they do not want to tilt the competitive playing field by revealing too much about who's in front and who's not.

One strategy we have seen top sellers use to gain insights into the mind of the customer is to rely on key advocates. They are already ostensibly in your corner, and if you've done your job well in cultivating them and helping them improve their influence, they can provide invaluable information.

If you're unable to learn firsthand how the customer sees things, then you will have to rely upon careful guesswork. What's the customer's buying history? How does the market perceive you and your competitors? What have other customers said about you? While this method is certainly more analytical than fortune-telling, it may prove in the end to be no more reliable. How unbiased can you be? Who else on your team can provide a balanced perspective on the situation?

Competitive Assessment—A Tool

The two parts of our competitive assessment are: 1) selection criteria and their level of importance, and 2) your customer's perception of your strengths and weaknesses when compared to the competition. The Competitive Assessment tool on the following page has proved valuable for our clients in carefully considering their competitive positions.

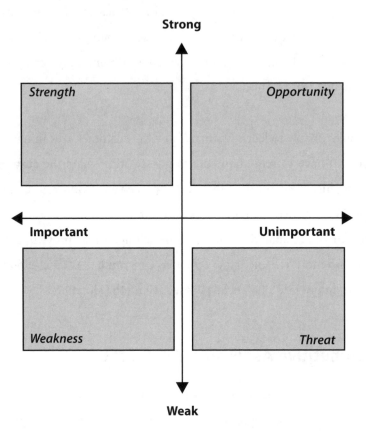

Competitive Position Scale

Strong

| Strength | | Opportunity |

Important ← → **Unimportant**

| Weakness | | Threat |

Weak

The goal of using a tool such as this is to develop a clear, visual picture of how your offering compares to your competitors. The tool can be used regardless of the number of competitors—or the types of competition—confronting you, because it focuses on selection criteria and your relative position of strength for each of those criteria.

Let's look at Diane's situation and use this tool to evaluate her competitive position.

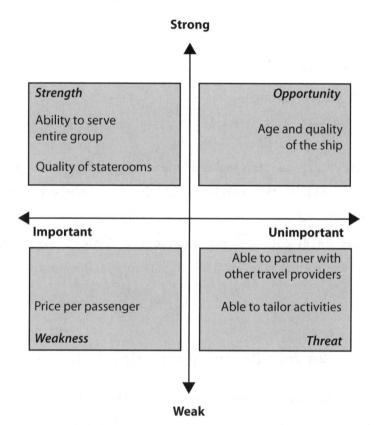

Strong

Strength	*Opportunity*
Ability to serve entire group	Age and quality of the ship
Quality of staterooms	

Important ←→ **Unimportant**

	Able to partner with other travel providers
Price per passenger	Able to tailor activities
Weakness	*Threat*

Weak

Our ultimate goal in understanding the SWOT of the competitive situation is to develop a sales approach that accomplishes the following:

- minimizes weaknesses

- emphasizes strengths

- exploits opportunities

- neutralizes threats.

Accurately completing this tool is a little more challenging than completing some of the other tools introduced thus far, simply because you have to get inside your customer's head to assess the situation accurately. However, simply putting words onto the tool is only the beginning of your competitive strategy. It's what you do with this information that matters.

Think Like Your Competition—Only in Reverse

As important as it is to get inside your customer's head—to think as your customer thinks—it is also important to think like your competitor. Your strength is their weakness, your opportunity their threat, and vice versa. The strategic approach you take with these strengths, weaknesses, opportunities, and threats ought to be weighed carefully against the strategy your competition is also trying to take. If you want to emphasize your strength, they want to hide their corresponding weakness. If you want to offset a threat, they are trying to capitalize on that opportunity.

Strengths

In our competitive analysis tool, strengths are those selection criteria that are considered important by your customer and in which you are considered to have an advantage over the competing alternatives. May we return to our friend Diane? In her case, there were two areas of strength. First was her company's ability to accommodate the customer's entire team for dining and meeting arrangements. Second was the quality of her cruise ship's staterooms. These attributes are important to this customer, and the customer believes that Diane's cruise line has greater capabilities in these two areas.

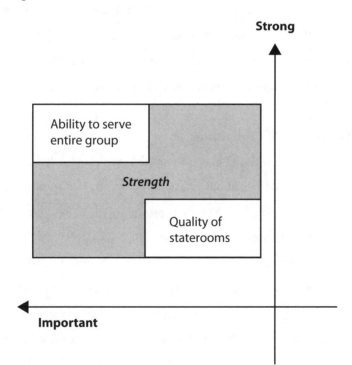

The greatest challenge when it comes to our strengths is holding our ground. One of the most common traps sellers fall into is complacency. Sellers often become complacent about their strengths by acting as though a customer's opinion will not shift or change over time. Remember, the competition is looking to displace us, to erode our strengths, or to offset them with strengths of their own.

Emphasizing our strengths by continuously "reselling" them to the customer is one approach. Most salespeople default to this approach because they are comfortable touting what they are good at. Who is not? The risk in this approach stems from human nature: We tend to discount the self-praise of others; it is too much special pleading. Not only do we discount it, we might even be offended. Overselling your strengths may have counterproductive effects on your customer.

What would your competitors attempt to do to overcome your competitive strengths? Some may attempt to discredit you. To what result? Well, how do you feel about politicians who attempt to discredit their opponents, or product manufacturers who speak badly about their competitors? Another approach that's taken is to persuade the customer to value the strength less—that is, to make the selection criterion less important, especially when compared to areas where the competitor is strong. Sometimes this is called *eclipsing*, which amounts to substituting one criterion for another on the customer's ranking scale.

For Diane, it was crucial that she continuously reinforced her strengths. We coached her to use a question-based approach to re-persuade her customer. For example, "You said stateroom quality is a critical selection criterion for this decision. Why is that so important to you?" And, "If you had to split the groups, what could some of the consequences be?" These types of questions reinforce in the customer's mind the importance of the strengths Diane's solution possesses.

Getting the customer to articulate their rationale is important for several reasons. The first, and perhaps most important reason, has to do with an old selling proverb: "If you say it, they can doubt it; but if they say it, it's true." The second reason has to do with ownership. When the customer expresses their rationale—when they specify why they want what they want—it is in their own words. They own it, therefore. They are then better able to communicate the rationale to others (to defend it, in other words).

Weaknesses

Those criteria that the customer sees as important, but where you are at a comparative disadvantage to your competition, are considered weaknesses. Diane's customer regarded price per passenger as very important, but Diane was weak in this regard.

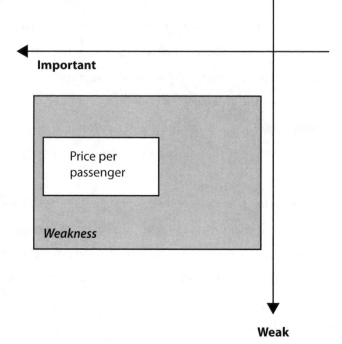

The challenge in dealing with a weakness is that it's difficult to make a customer care less about something that they feel strongly about. (Have you ever tried to persuade someone on the opposite side of the political aisle to care less about their favorite issues? How did that go?)

In Diane's case, price wasn't a top priority for the customer (remember the criteria ranking). Diane felt it was possible to overcome the weakness or work around it. We coached her in a couple of approaches. First, Diane could reinterpret the criterion in a way that favored her solution. This is done frequently in sales, any time someone gets us to consider "total cost of ownership" in place of simple price.

Diane's customer had defined price as the price each passenger will pay to be on board the cruise ship. This definition neglected to consider other components of what might be called the "cost of cruising." Diane considered amenities, transportation, convenience, and other aspects of her offering that could contribute to the customer's perception of "cost." Because reinterpreting is a fairly well-known tactic, customers may see it coming from miles away. If they smell a sales technique, they will likely put up some stiff resistance. On the other hand, we'd say its payoffs make the risk worth taking. We think it's important that you test the willingness of your customer to look at things in a different light, otherwise you may alienate them.

Another approach to dealing with a weakness is to lessen the value of the criterion to the customer. However, let us restate a grand caveat. If a customer has determined that something is important, it will almost always be difficult to make them think otherwise. Unfortunately, that is our challenge here: Persuade them to care less than they currently do.

A third approach is to persuade them that you are stronger than they realize. Or, you could simply strengthen your offering. Unfortunately, we all have weaknesses, and our customers generally know what they are. If the customer believes you're weak in one area, and they are correct, then you can try the two tactics mentioned above. But if the customer is wrong about you, and you're actually better at something than they believe, then it is about changing that perception by providing evidence to the contrary.

Opportunities

We have an opportunity when there is a selection criterion in which the customer believes that we are strong, but unfortunately doesn't care very much about it. This is a golden opportunity to create a competitive strength, if only the seller can make the customer value this criterion more. In many cases, customers consider certain criteria as low priorities simply because they haven't given them a great deal of thought. This means that if we can increase the customer's awareness of the importance of these criteria—that is, rethink their overall impact on the success of the initiative—then we may be able to persuade them to elevate its importance.

For our friend Diane, the greatest opportunity lay in the age and quality of her ships. The customer acknowledged that Diane was much stronger than her competitors in this area, but they did not regard the selection criterion as important. The challenge for Diane was to figure out if they had ranked this criterion lower because they simply had not thought much about it, or because they had.

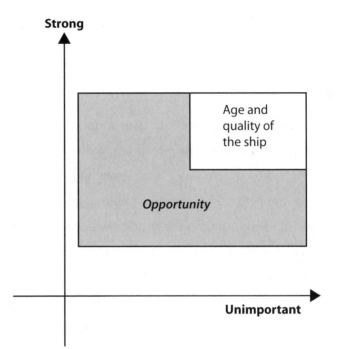

In Diane's case, the criterion's ranking owed more to ignorance than careful analysis. Once Diane began asking the customer questions, the tide turned. Questions included:

- What problems could result from a cruise provider whose ships appear dated or less than clean?

- How might it help you to choose a provider who invests in the quality of its ships?

When it comes to your opportunities, ask yourself how you can make your customer care.

Threats

Threats are merely the opposite side of opportunities. The customer doesn't care about the criterion, which is a good thing, because we are not perceived by the customer to be strong in this area. Unfortunately, if our competitor implements a well-thought-out competitive strategy, one in which he makes the customer care about the criterion, this threat evolves into an actual weakness. One common mistake we see salespeople make when confronted with the threat is to ignore it, ostrich-style. Maybe if we do not bring it up, they seem to think, it will go away of its own accord. This approach has its temptations. After all, if it's not important to the customer, why bring it up? Let sleeping dogs lie. Unfortunately, if you don't bring it up, who will? Well obviously, the competition will. So, how can you manage threats?

In the first place, you need to figure out a way to keep this criterion minimized. Sometimes this could involve dialog that allows the customer to articulate why the criterion is relatively unimportant. You might also direct the customer's attention toward another selection criterion. Beware of being lulled into a false sense of security around the attribute that the customer doesn't care about, because your competitor isn't likely to sit back and ignore this issue.

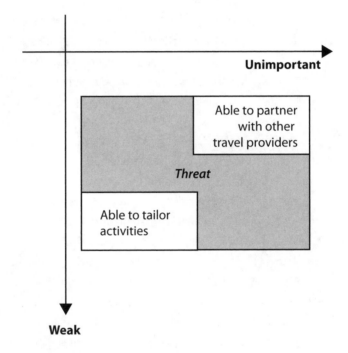

Chapter 5 Summary

Competitive analysis involves clear-eyed judgment, ruthless introspection, and unflinching candor. It involves what some philosophers call methodic doubt—test all assumptions, question hypotheses, seek answers. When you have your competitive picture, play to your strengths and offset your weaknesses.

In this chapter we offered advice on managing your competitors. The first step is defining who your competitors are. The next is understanding how your customers will evaluate you against them. Customers use prioritized selection criteria and compare each vendor's strengths and weaknesses relative to that list of criteria. A clear understanding of the customer's selection criteria will reveal where you are strong and where you are weak. The purpose of any SWOT analysis is to enable you to minimize your weaknesses, emphasize your strengths, capitalize on your opportunities, and neutralize threats. The reason this is significant in competitive analysis is because your strengths are likely to be your competitors' weaknesses, your opportunities their threats. Knowing where your competitors stand in relationship to your own strengths, weaknesses, opportunities, and threats will enable you to manage them more effectively.

Chapter 6

Quantifying Value

In July 2011 two bottles of liquid treasure, in this case French champagne, crossed half the globe, from The Åland Islands off the coast of Finland to a Russian restaurant in Singapore—Buyan Haute Cuisine and Caviar Bar. The restaurant paid $78,400 (or 54,000 €) in an online auction for these two special bottles, planning to display them in its wine museum, which already houses other rare wines. Why did the restaurant pay so much? Well, therein lies a tale, which explains why value truly is in the eye of the beholder.

"Come Quickly, I Am Drinking the Stars"

Champagne, which technically refers only to sparkling wine produced in the Champagne region of France, has been a favorite of the upwardly mobile for centuries. Dom Perignon (to whom the quote above is attributed), did not invent champagne, but he made so many significant contributions to its production that the wine named for him is some of the most expensive sold today. We cannot confirm, but we have it on good authority, that it is worth every penny. The wine that made its way from the Åland Islands to Singapore, however, was not Dom Perignon. So what explains the price tag?

In the summer of 2010, divers from Sweden and Åland discovered an as yet unexplored shipwreck off the Åland archipelago, in the Baltic Sea. There was nothing particularly remarkable about the ship itself: a two-masted schooner lying on its wooden hull in 200 feet of near-freezing water. The divers made some interesting archeological finds: plates, cookware, spices, coffee beans, and carpets. But none of that compared to the real treasure on the ship: 172 bottles of vintage champagne.

The name of this sunken treasure ship is still unknown, as is her destination, although speculation has it that she was bound for the royal court of the last Russian Tsar, Nicholas II, in St. Petersburg. According to experts, this champagne's vintage is from the first half of the 1800s, making it the oldest champagne in the world. The bottles did not have labels, but markings burned into the corks indicated that they were from the champagne houses of Veuve Clicquot, Juglar, and Heidsieck. Would you like to buy a bottle? Or two?

Although we're sure that many people believe it would be very cool to own such a unique piece of history, few of us personally know anyone who could rationalize such an extravagant expenditure (not even to celebrate an extremely important occasion!). But the restaurant in Singapore could. Why? What rationale did they give?

Frankly, we do not know, and it really does not matter. What matters is this significant point: Every decision people make to buy something—in fact, every decision at all—has a rationale to support it. Sometimes the rationale is carefully thought out and perfectly defensible. Other times, it is hastily devised, with questionable logic. But a rationale is there. It could be meeting fundamental needs, such as food, clothing, or shelter. Or it might be projecting a certain image or status through ownership of a luxury automobile or a particular brand of clothing. Even when we have a vigorously defensible rationale underlying a purchasing decision, we might still find ourselves asking if it was worth it.

Many of you reading this chapter probably have at least one good business suit. That suit could have cost you anywhere from $100 to $3,000—or maybe more. How much would you pay for a good suit? How much do you value the quality of the material? How important is the proper, custom fit? Is the label on the inside of the jacket important to you? In other words, how do you measure the suit's value?

What Is Value?

A widely-used measurement of value is depicted in the equation below:

$$Value = Benefits - Costs$$

In general, people will say "yes" to a purchase if the *sum* (that is, value) of the *minuend* (benefits) and *subtrahend* (costs) is a positive number (that is, if benefits are greater than costs). This measurement of value can be quantified, if you work the equation like an arithmetic problem. In fact, if you are selling a premium-priced product, you simply *must* quantify it.

Consider our sunken champagne as an example. What is the cost of the champagne? The Singapore restaurant paid $75,000 for those two vintage bottles. Is that the cost? Well, partly it is. But true cost comprises many elements in addition to the price, which is already in terms of quantity and therefore easily measured. For instance, the restaurant probably paid expert advisors to appraise the champagne and help them understand what they were getting into. Then there is the soft cost of time: time spent researching, time spent in the auction, and so forth. Once purchased, transportation costs must be considered. Once the champagne reached Buyan Haute Cuisine and Caviar Bar, it is likely that their insurance and security costs would have increased. We do not pretend to be experts here, but there are probably other soft drivers of cost in this scenario, which must be added to the hard driver of the price. But for simplicity's sake in this example, let's just consider true cost to be equal to price. If cost is $75,000, benefits must be *greater* than $75,000 for there to be positive value in this equation. If you are trying to persuade the owners of Buyan to buy the champagne, one of your tasks is to find benefits that are greater than $75,000.

Every salesperson has something to sell, be it a product or a service. And those products and services have price tags, which may or may not fluctuate in the transaction. We refer to these price tags as *concrete costs*. The concrete cost represents the fixed, out-of-pocket expense to purchase the product or service. But the concrete cost, as we stated above, is only one component of true cost. Other factors, which we categorize under the heading *abstract costs*, must also be accounted for.

Concrete and Abstract Costs

The champagne bottles cost the restaurant $75,000. That is the concrete cost, the money Buyan paid out of pocket. If the owners knew they were going to sell both bottles to, say, a collector for a total of $125,000, then Buyan would realize a concrete benefit (a hard dollar amount). In this case—with only these two values, concrete cost and concrete benefit— the final value in our equation would be a positive $50,000. Easy math, right? Unfortunately, it is seldom that simple or easy.

While certain elements of the *minuend* and *subtrahend* of any value equation are going to be simple and easy (for instance, figuring price as part of the concrete cost), others will be much more difficult to quantify. Of course, keeping it simple in this equation may not be the best, or most thorough, approach. If the value equation is to be complete, abstract values must also be quantified in a meaningful way.

What's This Really Going to Cost Me?

Abstract costs are those cost elements that are difficult to measure effectively. Risk is an excellent example of an abstract cost. Your customers face risk whenever making purchasing decisions—the bigger the purchase, the bigger the risk. It could take the form of reputational risk. What if they buy, but things go badly? What will people say? It could be professional risk. They decide to buy, but their boss is angered because she prefers another provider. There could be the risk of business disruption, such as learning a new process, which requires training and takes time, or installing new equipment, which may end up having reliability problems.

These risks, whatever they are, factor into the cost *subtrahend*. Think of our champagne buyer's difficult decision. "It is going to cost us $75K, and if it turns out to be a bad decision, we're going to be widely recognized as the ones who made it!" So how much additional weight does this contribute to the *subtrahend* of cost? That is a difficult question to answer because it's tricky to quantify risks. Is this particular risk a $10 risk or a $100,000 risk? Unfortunately, if you can't put a number on this abstract value then you can't complete the equation.

Risk is one example of an abstract cost element, but there are others. Previously, we mentioned things like hiring experts, transporting the champagne, installing tougher security, and buying more insurance. What if Buyan had to invest in a special holding room for the champagne? Or move inventory from one location to another in order to accommodate this new purchase? There are measureable costs affiliated with these modifications (not to mention hassles and headaches). How many times have you—or someone you know—backed away from a decision simply because it seemed like "too much trouble" or because the risk seemed too severe? We've all done that, and it's because we know that simple price does not equal true cost; other factors play a role.

Your customers ascribe worth to these abstract cost elements, even if they only do it informally in their heads. It's up to you to discover what that worth is. By gaining a complete understanding of how the customer chalks up concrete and abstract costs, you can begin to see what you're up against when it comes to establishing the worth of the benefits. Your sales strategy can then incorporate an approach from one of two directions: You can either adjust the worth of the *subtrahend* (that is, reduce the costs); or you can adjust the worth of the *minuend* (that is, increase the benefits). The former will likely cost you something, while the latter will cost you nothing but effort (and no small sales skills).

What's My ROI?

In our champagne example, Buyan saw benefits (concrete and abstract) exceeding $75,000. As already mentioned, the restaurant could have plans to sell the bottles to a customer for a profit, which provides a very concrete benefit (and a positive value, as we showed). But let's assume that isn't the case, and that instead the restaurant plans to hold the bottles in their wine museum. What are the benefits?

Certainly, winning the auction resulted in international notoriety. People from around the world now knew about Buyan. We imagine there might be some with the means to make special pilgrimages to the champagne shrine. But even locally, the addition to the wine museum would likely yield foot traffic. And wouldn't all those visitors be potential restaurant customers? Buyan would have ample business, probably with demand exceeding their supply. Market economics, of course, teaches us that scarcity drives up prices. So Buyan would potentially see more business, at higher margins, because of their investment. They likely considered answers to questions like, "How many additional diners will come to the restaurant because of the publicity?" And "How much additional revenue and profit will these diners bring?" They probably also thought about how long the effects of the publicity would last.

Formal return-on-investment (ROI) studies, established payback periods, or net present value studies are a few examples of measurements that companies use to evaluate investment decisions. If a company can complete these equations, it can also complete the value equation, because the same elements exist. If your value equation won't end positively, neither will these other evaluations.

Is This Fuzzy Math?

In the 2000 presidential election, George W. Bush coined the phrase "fuzzy math" to describe the economic analysis used by his opponent, Al Gore. It is commonly used today to describe math calculations that are debatable or questionable. Some of us may have even had customers accuse us of "fuzzy math" when we proposed a quantified value our solution would provide (in some cases, they might have been right). But the days of "fuzzy math" ought to go the way of the hanging chad. The single best way to get customers to accept your value equation is to get them to collaborate with you on the calculations. As the old sales proverb says: "If you say it, they doubt it; but if they say it, it's true."

As we've shown, part of an effective sales strategy is demonstrating a positive final value to the value equation. A step in that process is gaining a clear understanding of how the customer defines—and quantifies—the costs of your solution. A second step is working with the customer to define and quantify the benefits of your solution. You should notice that the word "customer" is in both statements. You could make your best guess as to how your customer will rationalize their purchasing decision (or lack thereof). Unfortunately, our experience tells us that salespeople have a tendency to *over*state the benefits their solutions bring and *under*state how the customer would define costs.

Naturally, all that's required to prevent this tendency is a simple conversation between you and your customer, right? Except it's never truly simple. It is, however, unavoidable. Among the many challenges you will face is that your customer may not be able to quantify the costs and benefits of your solution. If they can't do this, the completeness of your value equation may suffer. Rendering a good decision from a thinly constructed value equation is difficult. As any mathematician or statistician (or long-serving CFO) will tell you, decision making is about minimizing variables so that you understand the situation as clearly as possible.

A Real Example, Please

Kevin took a class on pricing models while enrolled in the Executive MBA program at UNC-Chapel Hill. His professor challenged the students by claiming that there was no such thing as a commodity (defined as a product that is supplied without qualitative differentiation across a market, and whose primary characteristic is substitutability). Pricing was unique to the value of the product, argued the professor.

Students were quick to try to debunk the professor's claim with examples of true commodities. "Salt!" yelled one student. "Water!" yelled another. "Wrong and wrong," replied the professor. "You can buy a 25 lb. bag of Morton's table salt for $8.00; while a 9 oz. jar of Himalayan Pink Artesian salt costs $10.00." For those keeping score at home, that is $0.02 for an ounce of Morton's salt compared to more than $1.00 for an ounce of the Himalayan salt. What's the difference? Well, there may be many (and we have friends who will tell us there surely are significant differences), but for our purposes, the primary difference is that someone will pay more for Himalayan than for Morton. It's "the eye of the beholder" concept at work again. Is the value scale working in this case? We think it is.

We have a client that manufactures and sells a small piece of equipment to hospitals. The device is considered a commodity by most hospital purchasing departments. Our client's product costs nearly 20 times what hospitals currently pay for a competitive product. So let's say our client's product cost $20 per unit, whereas their competitors sell a cheaper version, albeit a less effective substitute, for about $19 less per unit. This is a big disparity. And because hospitals purchase hundreds, if not thousands, of these small devices, the price difference can add up pretty quickly.

Let's say that a hospital intends to purchase 1,000 units. The total outlay on the cheap substitute would be $1,000. For our client's version, the tab is $20,000. That delta between the two products represents a concrete cost of $19,000 (because they have to buy one or the other product as a necessary tool of their operations). The product attributes of both devices are similar, but the more expensive device has two added features, which have proven to reduce infection cases by at least 20 percent. The particular infection that the device can prevent is not very common. In fact, for every 1,000 units of this device purchased and used, a hospital might have only 15 occurrences of this particular infection. The problem is that this infection is quite expensive for a hospital, with an average cost of $50,000 per case, none of which is re-imbursable by governmental or insurance organizations. By investing an additional $19,000 (concrete cost), the hospital could potentially eliminate three cases, thereby saving at least $150,000 (concrete bene-fits) by not having to treat as many patients who acquire this infection.

Value	Benefits	Costs
$150K - $20K = $130K	3 fewer infection cases per year at a cost of $50K per infection = **$150K**	**$19K** excess paid for product
Unknown—but quantifiable	Better patient outcomes (abstract)	Lost productivity during training period (abstract)
Unknown—but quantifiable	Improved reputation because of reduced infections and better patient outcomes (abstract)	Reluctance to learn a new product (abstract)

As you can see from the chart, there are abstract costs involved in this case as well. For example, there is the cost of change, which means (among other things) training staff on the new product, lost staff productivity during the training period, the hassle of migrating from the old product to the new one, and potentially angering and alienating some clinicians who may be resistant to the new product. Each element could potentially be measured and quantified, resulting in higher costs. So our subtrahend is actually well beyond the original $19,000 price tag.

But there are also abstract benefits. Because the infection prevented by this device is very detrimental to a patient's health, eliminating—or even just reducing—instances of that infection not only saves the hospital money (when it doesn't have to treat the patients), but improves the quality of care received by the patients. This alone eliminates many health complications and leads to shorter hospital stays, better patient outcomes, and improved healthcare availability. Each of these elements can also be turned into quantified benefits to add to the $150,000 benefit the hospital would get by reducing this particular infection by three patients per year.

Another Real Case Study

Let's look at quantifying value from another business perspective. One of our clients is a global manufacturer of medical lasers. Their lasers are used for many different purposes, from blasting kidney stones, to corrective eye surgery, to hair removal. A couple of years ago, this company launched a new laser, specifically designed for hair removal. This new laser cost $90,000, compared to the previous model, which sold for $60,000. As you can imagine, selling this newer laser for a 50 percent premium in price was going to be no easy task, particularly when the target customer base was made up of smaller, less cash-flush dermatology clinics.

Mike was a very successful sales rep for our client. He had been selling lasers to dermatologists and plastic surgeons for years. He was particularly successful in selling his laser's capability in hair removal. Neither of us has personally ever had this procedure performed, but from what we understand, it can be a fairly long and painful process, not much different from cattle branding (or pulling out fingernails?). In fact, it's not uncommon for men who have large target areas, such as the back, to come for their first treatment and never return for their next four, because the procedure was too painful. We were told by one laser technician that she has finally found a way to bring big burly hairy men to tears. We were not amused. Well, we were *slightly* amused, but only because we did not envision ourselves coming under her ministrations. As you can imagine, getting a patient to return for future treatments often takes a lot of skill on behalf of the dermatologists and the cosmetic staff.

The new laser launched by Mike's company had some unique capabilities. First, the new laser made the procedure much quicker because it could cover a larger surface area in a shorter amount of time. Secondly, and most importantly, the new laser was practically painless. Mike was excited about both of these new capabilities, but he still worried that he would find it difficult to justify the price differential.

Within a month of the new product launch, Mike began working with Dr. Bennett. Dr. Bennett had a six-year-old laser he had been using for hair removal. When the doctor had purchased his existing laser, he had great hopes for the hair removal portion of his practice—and things had started out well. However, over the previous two years, the number of clients seeking out this procedure had dropped and Dr. Bennett started focusing his practice on alternative revenue streams. Mike thought the doctor might be an ideal prospect for this new laser and suspected it might help to rejuvenate his hair removal business.

In Mike's initial investigation, Dr. Bennett told him that he owned his existing laser outright, and would only consider purchasing a new unit if he could sell his old laser to someone else. Mike overcame the doctor's initial resistance by telling him that he could find a buyer for his existing laser, if he was willing to sell it for $40,000. Dr. Bennett thought about Mike's offer, but said that he was still unsure. "I don't know, Mike," he said. "I would still have to come up with an additional

$50,000 to get the new laser, and I am not sure I could justify the additional expense. That is a lot of money for us to spend."

So to help Dr. Bennett quantify the value of the new laser, Mike went back to our formula, *Value = Benefits – Costs*. Mike first began by identifying the concrete and abstract costs of purchasing a new laser. While the price of the new laser was $90,000, Mike was confident he could sell Dr. Bennett's old unit for $40,000. This made his concrete cost $50,000. Mike then turned his attention to potential abstract costs.

Mike identified three critical abstract costs about which Dr. Bennett might be concerned. First was the risk of spending $50,000 and not receiving the anticipated return on investment. Second was the hassle of retraining the staff on the new product. This was a real concern because the aestheticians were used to the existing laser. Getting them to embrace a new tool might prove difficult. How might they react? What if they didn't like the new laser? And finally, there were the implications of allocating so much of his existing capital for this purchase. There were many competing priorities, and Dr. Bennett might see this as a sort of zero-sum game. For example, the office administrator had been promised a lobby makeover, but with the purchase of a new laser, the makeover would have to wait. Mike knew he would have to test his ideas against what Dr. Bennett might really be thinking. But before he met with him, Mike knew that he had to be prepared to outweigh the doctor's costs with concrete and abstract benefits. So what were the benefits of the new laser?

Mike had some background information that might help his case. He knew that Dr. Bennett's office averaged 10 patients per month who sought laser hair removal. And 50 percent of those patients coming in for this procedure would not return after the first visit because it was too painful. Mike also knew that the office had four aestheticians who would spend approximately one hour working with each patient.

Armed with this information, Mike first figured that one of the concrete benefits from purchasing the new laser was that each aesthetician would be able to see three times as many patients in that same hour because the new laser made possible a quicker procedure. Taking an average laser hair removal cost of $200 per visit, and multiplying that time across the four aestheticians and the increased number of patients, Bennett had an increased revenue potential of about $1,600 per day. Mike also estimated that, with the relative painlessness of the new laser, the practice could reduce attrition by 50 percent, though he suspected that number might be much higher. That could potentially improve Bennett's revenue by an additional $4,000 per month.

Mike was fairly confident that his concrete benefits alone might persuade Dr. Bennett to buy the new laser; however, to be thorough, he carefully considered the abstract benefits of his solution. One of the abstract benefits he identified was a happier aesthetician staff. Most aestheticians didn't like the stress and anguish of doing an hour-long procedure that was painful for the patient. Mike also thought the aestheticians would then be likelier to upsell other procedures—after all, if they were all quick and painless, it was an easier sell. He imagined they could promote hair removal during, say, a Botox procedure, even while the patient was in the chair.

Mike was now ready to meet with Dr. Bennett. He felt he would be able to successfully quantify the value of purchasing the new laser. Dr. Bennett opened the meeting by telling Mike that he had discussed the new laser with his business partner, and they didn't see how a $50,000 investment could be justified at the time. Fortunately, because Mike had done his homework, he could walk through the value equation conversation with Dr. Bennett and make a compelling case for his solution. He began by asking Dr. Bennett about the new laser's costs. Dr. Bennett talked about the need to capture his return-on-investment within 24 months, he mentioned the hassle of training his four aestheticians, and he worried about breaking his promise to his office manager regarding a lobby makeover. Essentially, he confirmed Mike's own speculations about the abstract cost factors. Like any effective seller (or at least ones we have trained), Mike asked questions and listened to Dr. Bennett's answers. Then he asked follow-up questions and continued to listen. While he listened, he began to hear Dr. Bennett quantifying his own benefits. They talked about patient throughput, patient retention, and upselling potential.

By the end of the conversation, Dr. Bennett realized that without any new marketing, he could recover his investment of $50,000 within 16 months, substantially better than the 24-month ROI he said was an essential minimum. If Dr. Bennett put some additional time and effort into marketing his new quick and painless hair removal service, he might even be able to reduce his ROI time down to eight months!

Mike closed the deal with Dr. Bennett. He realized he never would have been able to get it done if he had not first carefully considered the concrete and abstract costs and benefits.

What's the Lesson in All of This?

Our challenge as salespeople is to convince our customers that our products are worth buying. We not only have to show that the customer's problem is worth solving, but that our solution, when compared to our competitors, is a *better* solution. We may not be considered the "low-cost provider" in our markets, so naturally price is an objection frequently encountered. It's not that our customers won't buy a more expensive solution. It's just that they want to make sure there is justification for any investment they may make. So quantifying the value of our solution is critical. The value equation is our not-so-secret weapon in this effort. It helps us tell and sell our story to our customers.

In our laser hair removal case, we had a knowledgeable doctor, someone who knew the value of a new patient and of happier staff. However, not everyone you speak with is going to have the ability—or perhaps even the willingness—to quantify all of the costs or benefits associated with your solution, whether abstract or concrete. You will need to collect that information throughout the process, as you meet with key players in your prospect's organization. The next time you hear that some capability of your solution might save them time, ask them how much time. The next time a customer says, "My team is really going to be disappointed if we don't do this," ask, "How will you measure the impact of that?" It's about quantifying what you can, when you can. And next time a customer asks you, "Where did you come up with that number?" be sure to have an answer.

Chapter 6 Summary

Every customer has unique qualifications for what they consider to be valuable. Consequently, a formula that helps us quantify that value is

Value = Benefits – Cost

Simply put, if the benefits outweigh the costs, the value is sufficient to justify the purchase. However, it's not really so simple. In this chapter, we discussed how both benefits and costs can be calculated in either abstract or concrete terms. In quantifying value, it is important, therefore, to understand both the concrete and the abstract measures of benefits and costs. What's probably most important in all of this is not what you think those costs and benefits are, but what your customer thinks they are. Just as beauty is in the eye of the beholder, value is in the perspective of the customer. So we not only have to show that the customer's problem is worth solving, but also that our solution, when compared to our competitors, is worth buying.

Chapter 7

Pipeline Management

This scene is an all-too-recognizable one. A sales manager somewhere is talking pipeline with one of her sales reps. It's a conversation that takes place at least monthly and has the eerie familiarity of déjà vu. It might go something like this:

Sales Rep: Yes, I believe we'll close the KNG deal by the end of the month for $250,000, as well as MRG for an additional $125,000.

Manager: C'mon. You've been predicting KNG will close for six months. I'll believe it when I see it!

You could insert almost any customer, set the story in almost any industry, with any sales rep and manager, and the conversation would still be essentially the same. Shareholders want accurate forecasts. Management wants accurate forecasts. And salespeople usually do their best to supply them. And yet, it seems that forecasts are often inaccurate, sometimes wildly so. From every sector, in company after company, from seller to seller, we see this same problem occurring. We've found some very simple reasons why forecasts aren't always reliable.

"There's a Pony in There Somewhere..."

Most salespeople have a deep reservoir of optimism in their bodies. It's what sustains them in the face of constant rejection. It's what helps them overcome obstacles. It's what allows them to take the lemon they have just been handed, and open up a thriving lemonade stand.

This constant optimism so frequently found in salespeople reminds us of the old joke about the dad who wants to teach his optimistic son that life is not always a bowl of cherries or a bed of roses. So instead of presents under his Christmas tree, the boy finds a pile of horse manure. Imagine Dad's surprise when little Jimmy lets out an excited whoop and begins running around the house looking in closets and the backyard. "What are you doing, Jimmy?" Jimmy's reply is in classic sales-speak: "With that much manure, there's got to be a pony in here somewhere!"

Sometimes our sales pipelines look rosier than they should because we believe there's a pony in there among the manure. Misguided optimism is often to blame for sales mis-forecasting.

"Good Morning, Pooh. If It Is a Good Morning, Which I Doubt."

Who doesn't love Eeyore? A.A. Milne's beloved but gloomy donkey is hard to resist. We know he must be popular amongst some salespeople because, despite the indefatigable optimism of many, there is the occasional seller whose forecasts sound as though he is channeling him. A sales Eeyore in a strategy meeting might sound like this:

"Don't have much going on this quarter."

"Smith Companies probably won't close."

"We are very reliant on one guy; I would not be surprised if he got reassigned."

"Abco is probably going to delay until next fiscal year, and I would not be shocked if they went with our competition. Not that it matters."

In our consulting work in the area of forecasting, we've found that it's not just the cock-eyed optimists who screw up their forecasts. Some sellers, when confronted with the optimists' pile of horse manure, would typically shrug and say it's what they expected. Like Milne's famous donkey, they see the glass as not just half empty, but as continually leaking.

Of course, the doom-and-gloom forecast may be inspired less by a gloomy temperament—or cynicism or even realism—than it is by self-preservation. The sandbagger who downplays his forecast, after all, lowers expectations all around. Instead of seeing gold in "them thar hills," these Eeyores remind everyone how difficult the gold is to extract or how thoroughly mined the hills already are. These gloomy voices would rather keep their forecasts quiet and conservative. No bold promises from them.

This reminds us of another old joke. A guy in church tells his minister he's going to give up drinking. The minister turns and walks toward the pulpit, causing the old man to ask, "Where are you going, Preacher?" To which the minister replies, "To tell the congregation." The man, in a panic, shrieks, "Don't do it, Preacher! Then I'd have to quit for sure!" Putting our name to a forecast is like making a promise over an outcome we do not directly control. It's uncomfortable. And too many things can turn the "sure thing" into a dead thing.

Step on a Crack...

Other salespeople may display a certain reticence in discussing the deals coming to fruition in their pipeline because of deep-seated superstitions. They're afraid that making an optimistic forecast will jinx the opportunity. So they are reluctant to say much about it, the way baseball players avoid talking to a pitcher who's throwing a no-hitter.

Of course, when this superstition is examined a bit more closely, we find that it is based on some sound logic. We have worked with many sellers whose greatest worry is that their manager will helicopter into a deal to "move it forward." Late involvement of management may occasionally add to the momentum of an opportunity, but more often, this practice is counterproductive. Customers do not always respond favorably to the heavy guns being rolled out, likening it to the car dealer who turns you over to the manager for closing the sale. However, there seems to be a strong correlation between a manager's early involvement in—and familiarity with—a customer, and the manager's ability to positively influence the decision. Sellers who practice "pipeline reticence" are likely worried about the helicopter manager who flies in, raises a lot of dust and noise, and then flies out while the customer runs for cover.

It's the Process, Stupid, or the Process Is Stupid

The science of human performance technology teaches us that performance problems in the workplace generally boil down to three overarching factors: attitude, skills, and knowledge. Attitude has to do with whether the workers want to do the task; it's the *why*. Skills, of course, are about ability; they are the *how*. And knowledge is about understanding; we might call that the *what*. When workers are not satisfactorily performing the tasks that are required, it boils down to gaps in the why, how, and what, and the interplay between the three of them. However, when it comes to complex tasks demanded of an entire enterprise (for example, pipeline management for a large-scale sales force), a fourth element becomes the *sine qua non* of good forecasting: a well-thought-out, validated, and repeatable process. And it's been our experience that many sellers—and many organizations—simply lack a reliable and consistent way to predict which deals will close and when. Producing an accurate forecast becomes a sort of meteorological art, but without the reliability. It's no wonder sellers resist doing them. And it's no wonder managers are frustrated. Nobody's getting what they really want or need out of the effort. To borrow a phrase used in reengineering and Total Quality Management (TQM), blame the process, not the people.

We know many of you are thinking that the only purpose of the pipeline process is so that senior sales leaders can keep track of who's working and who's not. More than one salesperson has expressed sentiments like this IT client manager's: "Forecasting has no value to me as a sales rep. My manager just wants it so he has something to hold over my head until the end of the month." We suspect that this is truer than managers may care to admit. Yet the reason this is the case is that bad information from bad pipeline management processes yield forecasts that have little value for anyone, except as an enforcement tool. However, there is tremendous value in managing your customer opportunities in an active pipeline management process. Emerging customer relationship management (CRM) software, such as SalesForce.com, Saleslogix, Siebel, and others, have made great strides in simplifying the reporting process. This ought to have led to better forecasts and improved pipeline management. Yet the problems have persistently survived, and sales reps and managers still have challenges getting the results everyone wants.

The obstacle stems from this simple truth: Good technology layered over processes that do not work yields unsatisfactory results. It would be like putting a Formula One engine into a Conestoga wagon. Too often companies implement a sales pipeline (or sales funnel) process into their organization to match their shiny new CRMs, without any regard to the core strategic sales activities that sales reps should be completing throughout the entire process.

Most pipeline or funnel management systems use terms such as Stage 1, Stage 2, Stage 3, and Stage 4, or the even more vague "Early Cycle," "Mid-Cycle," and "Late Cycle." We have seen five-stage models. We have seen seven-stage models. We have even seen a 12-stage model (whose stages closely mirrored 12-step programs, which was really pretty interesting and may deserve a book in its own right—but we digress). We do not think it matters very much how many stages the process has; five seems to be a pretty common "magic number," but our evidence tends to be anecdotal and experiential, rather than statistically significant. The problems arise not from the number of stages there are, but rather murkiness around each stage's definition. If for one constituency Stage 1 means "targeting and qualifying," but for another it means "uncovering needs," the pipeline's results will be ambiguous at best. A process whose boundaries and stage definitions can shift from constituency to constituency, or case by case, is a process that does not work. But when a clearly-defined pipeline process aligns perfectly with sales activities, the results can be stunning.

When the Pipeline Hums

We saw this success story play out while working with a global blood diagnostics instrument company. Jeff was their North American VP of Sales, and he was striving valiantly to improve his team's forecasting. After building a more rigorous pipeline process, not only did he get a more accurate sales forecast, but also an added benefit of a more strategically-minded sales team. Let us explain.

Jeff's North American sales team consisted of nearly 400 sales reps and their 75 sales managers. Like many organizations, forecasting was about as accurate as guessing when a double zero would come up on the roulette table. Sales reps didn't have an effective or consistent way to predict when their opportunities would close. Each region had its own way of doing things. This caused many problems for Jeff, to say nothing of his company. His biggest concern was providing a more accurate sales forecast to his board of directors each quarter. If projections were off by more than 5 percent in either direction, Jeff had to explain and justify it, a verbal shuffle that resembled a rhetorical *Riverdance*. He asked us to help him develop a pipeline process that would consistently meet the demand to provide accurate forecasts to the board.

We began the project with data collection. We interviewed Jeff's top-performing regional sales directors, sales managers, and account managers across the customer-facing enterprise. We wanted to learn three things. First, we had a hunch that those top performers did a better job of communicating to Jeff about how a customer was progressing toward a decision. What we wanted to know was how that communication process worked. Second, we wanted to know how they defined the stages or steps in the process. What sort of ground rules were they using to move customers out of one stage and into another? Third, we wanted to know what managers were doing to be a value-adding resource throughout the process.

At the time, the company did not have a centrally established, centrally controlled pipeline process across the enterprise. Some regions did it one way, some did it another. But among the top performers, there emerged a consistent theme. These top performers utilized a consistent and rigorous process for their region, whether it involved five pipeline stages, or three or four or 10, and they communicated frequently about opportunities' progress—or lack thereof—through the pipeline's stages.

The unfortunate reality, though, was that the top performers were not any more successful at forecasting than average or below-average performers were. For Jeff, this was not acceptable. So working in collaboration with a cross-functional team, we designed and implemented a rigorous, workable five-stage sales pipeline. The five stages were:

STAGE 1	STAGE 2	STAGE 3	STAGE 4	STAGE 5
Opportunity Qualification	Needs Development	Solution Identification	Implementation Resolution	Contract Confirmation

To be honest, Jeff was not impressed with the five stages. He actually said, "Seriously? I paid you guys how much and this is what you deliver? I could have gotten this myself from any sales strategy book." We did not really blame him for his first reaction (there is something wonderful about a client who speaks his mind). And really, in one significant way he was right. Our five stages were not delivered on stone tablets from Sinai. They were not particularly innovative. They were just five stages, with no magic attached to the number five.

There was, however, power in the model's simplicity, especially as things like scalability, applicability, and repeatability were considered. If your pipeline model is so complex you need to hire engineers to make sense of it, it will become useless. Our five stages had the advantage of being so simple that anyone can understand and use it. Another advantage of our model was the clarification of the boundaries between the stages themselves. What did impress Jeff—and what made this approach different from some of the company's flavor-of-the-week approaches from their past—was the clear and unambiguous way in which the five stages were delineated, and the key milestones and metrics built into each stage.

Agreeing upon the number of stages in your sales pipeline—and naming them in a way that is both memorable and denotative—is indeed a critical first step, but it is only the first step. More important than fixing on the right number of stages is clearly defining each of them. What constitutes the first stage? And how is it distinct from the second? What criteria have to be met to move an opportunity from Stage 3 to Stage 4? What key milestones have to be passed? What activities have to take place?

These criteria—the activities and milestones—ought to reflect the day-to-day selling life of the customer-facing enterprise. Is making contact at the C-level a necessary activity? If so, it ought to be a milestone ("Met with C-level buyers and identified company's goals") in one of the stages. Is mapping all the key players important to your team (and if it's not, please go back and reread chapter 3)? The completion of a Key Player Map ought to be an activity in one of the stages.

So, coupled closely with naming and defining each stage is ensuring that the pipeline process itself is integrated with the day-to-day activities in the sales process. That is, selling activities should *fit* with the pipeline. This connecting of the dots for Jeff's company gave them a process that was workable for the entire customer-facing enterprise, leading to positive changes in Jeff's forecasting accuracy.

Establishing the crucial criteria for each stage makes it easier for salespeople and managers to communicate with clarity where they are in the pipeline process. When Harry tells Sally that Company X is a Stage 3 opportunity, Sally knows that each of the criteria in Stages 1 and 2 have been met. With a bit of Q&A between her and Harry, she will know how close X is to graduating to Stage 4. She will probably also have an idea how likely X is to close, and perhaps even be able to estimate when.

Fire Rube Goldberg

Rube Garrett Lucius Goldberg was an American cartoonist, among many other things. You probably know him from his series of popular cartoons depicting ridiculously complex gadgets that perform simple tasks in indirect, convoluted ways. The cartoons struck a chord with many (we've all witnessed real-life Rube Goldberg machines at some point)—so much so that there are actually contests that challenge participants to make a complex machine to perform a simple task. Rube Goldberg machines are extraordinarily entertaining. But that kind of approach makes for a lousy pipeline planning process.

Many companies, however, seem intent on developing a sales pipeline process that would make Goldberg proud. It seems that in the corporate world, simplicity is a bad sign. If it's simple, it must not be complete. If it can be explained by mere mortals instead of the High Priests from the Temple of Engineering (or IT or Finance), it's probably not good enough. This explains a bit of our friend Jeff's response to our simple five-stage pipeline model. But it's important to remember that simplicity is crucial with processes that need to be scaled across large enterprises.

An effective pipeline process needs to combine simplicity with effectiveness; it not only must be easy to learn and apply across a population of users, it must be robust enough to stand up to day-to-day sales rigors. As we've discussed, the challenge is in thoroughly defining each stage, delineating them from one another, and clearly distinguishing their boundaries. The key task in this endeavor is identifying the proper milestones within each stage. The milestones comprise the tasks that must be completed before moving on. What comes before what? For example, it has been well established that it's important to understand early in the sales process who the key players are in the account, and what their roles are in the decision. A subsequent step might involve defining the customer's selection criteria.

I Can See Clearly Now:
A Fully-Functional Pipeline

Let's go back to Jeff's situation. We ended up developing a five-stage pipeline process that included critical milestones and tasks for each phase of the process. On the following page is Jeff's pipeline process as we designed it.

STAGE 1	STAGE 2	STAGE 3	STAGE 4	STAGE 5
Opportunity Qualification	Needs Development	Solution Identification	Implementation Resolution	Contract Confirmation
All players involved in decision process identified	Needs and downside risks identified	Financial buyer contacted	Implementation risks identified and addressed	Hard copy PO received
Identified advocates and adversaries	Strategy to neutralize adversaries implemented	Decision criteria validated	Reconfirmed with advocates that all outstanding issues are handled	Paperwork sent to Order Entry
Decision factors identified	Confirmed where buyer is in decision process	Buyers understand link between final solution and their needs	Confirmed that stakeholders have taken ownership for solution	Confirmed the purchase and delivery process
Nature and level of severity of buyer concern identified	Decision criteria identified	Competitive analysis completed; strategy for influencing decision criteria defined	Final presentation made to decision team	Training schedule and application assessment has been approved
	Compelling reason to act identified	"Go/No Go" decision discussed with customer		Implementation plan confirmed
	Availability of estimated budget confirmed			

Implementing this pipeline process had five distinct advantages for Jeff and his company:

1. **Account managers are clear about their call objective before the sales call begins.** Too often average performers walk in and out of their customers' offices without doing anything strategic to drive the customer closer to a decision. With clear milestones in each stage of the pipeline process, Jeff's team was able to check which milestones had not been passed for that stage, and then develop smart call plans to achieve those objectives. For example, if an account manager has an opportunity in Stage 3, and one of the milestones is to validate the customer's decision criteria, then the call objective is clear.

2. **It shortens the sales cycle.** Top account managers are proactively driving their customers' buying processes, versus playing a passive or reactive role. Having smart and clear milestones at each stage fosters momentum-building activities because account managers are motivated to get the customers to take action.

3. **The sales rep and his managers have absolute clarity about where the opportunity is in the pipeline.** An opportunity cannot move into Stage 3 until it has met all the criteria for Stage 2. And a rep cannot promote an opportunity to an advanced stage before its time, so nobody gets false optimism about a deal's likeliness to close.

4. **Sales managers can now quickly identify where a sales rep may need help.** Too often sales managers spend hours conducting "account reviews" with their teams without having any clear objectives for the conversation.

Establishing criteria for each stage of the pipeline process allows the manager to quickly identify which accounts seem to be "stuck" in the pipeline. They can collaborate with their reps on developing action plans to move the opportunity forward. Without milestones in each stage of the pipeline, managers may conduct account reviews with good intentions, but they can't establish which direction the seller should move to secure the business opportunity.

5. **Establishing clear milestones in each stage of the pipeline process creates a set of forecast metrics that senior sales leaders can rely on.** If the senior sales leaders can get their entire team working towards achieving the key milestones throughout the pipeline process, they will be more able to establish accurate forecasts that allow the operations, manufacturing, and finance departments to make better business decisions for the company.

The pipeline model we designed for Jeff quickly improved the company's forecasting accuracy, to say nothing of the sales team's increased interest in living the process. Jeff and his sales managers became more attuned to warning signs of an opportunity stalling or slowing. Conversely, they were able to respond more appropriately when an opportunity's forward momentum increased (because they saw it coming). Over time, Jeff and his management team established reliable metrics that gave them insights into their business. For instance, they learned that opportunities that entered Stage 3 had a 78 percent chance of closing. When the opportunity moved into Stage 4, the percentage jumped to 86 percent. So Jeff was able to provide his board of directors and other stakeholders, like the manufacturing and finance departments, the accurate forecast they were demanding. More importantly, his account managers and sales managers had a consistent pipeline process, one that was linked to their day-to-day selling tasks. For them, managing the complex sale became much less "Rube Goldbergian." It's enough to make Eeyore smile.

Chapter 7 Summary

Sales forecasting is inevitably problematic. Some salespeople are too optimistic. Some are too pessimistic. And beyond optimism and pessimism is plain, old forecasting ineptitude. The end result is forecasts that are inaccurate. This chapter provided some tools and techniques for improving your pipeline management process by helping you see the importance of building critical milestones into each stage. These milestones help create a common understanding of the pipeline process.

We propose that prospects in your pipelines can be categorized into five basic stages. We've found through experience that these five tend to work across nearly every conceivable sales sector. They are opportunity qualification, needs development, solution identification, implementation resolution, and contract confirmation.

You may incorporate more or less than five stages in your pipeline model. But more important than determining how many stages there should be is defining what criteria you use to promote a prospect from one stage to the next. These criteria need to be clearly defined and consistent across the entire customer-facing enterprise and in each sales opportunity. Without this consistency the pipeline falls apart, and so does the forecast. We also recommend that you err on the side of simplicity rather than complexity in developing your pipeline process.

Chapter 8

Developing a Sales Coaching Strategy

As performance improvement professionals, our clients have invited us to work with their sales teams on a variety of sales effectiveness challenges. Over the years we have worked with sales professionals of every skill level, learning from our experiences with all of them. We have worked with them to improve their call planning and execution skills. We have helped our clients successfully launch new products and pursue suitable customers. We have also worked with them to increase their proficiency in the more complex areas of opportunity, account, and territory management. It is this last objective at which we have aimed with this book, a project we originally conceived as a way to codify and disseminate many of the lessons learned and best practices observed over the years. It is our hope that this project will help sales reps better analyze opportunities and develop smart strategic opportunity plans to beat out the competition and win the business.

As managers ourselves, we know how books like this sometimes get used. Some folks will embrace these ideas, in whole or in part, and begin implementing them straightaway. Ironically, this book is not really meant for them; they are top performers because they are already doing much of what we describe. Another constituency may read this book, but choose to disregard the ideas completely. Although they may have the most to gain from implementing these "success ideas," they are the ones least likely to use them. However, it is neither the top performer nor the bottom performer who we had in mind when we conceived this book. Rather, it is that lot in the middle, the ones who often hit their numbers, but seem to have room for growth. They win some and lose some, like most salespeople, but they ought to be winning more than they are. It is this group of "middle performers" who represent our intended audience. We might call them the *coachable middle*. As a sales manager, it is likely that you know who on your team falls into this group. And because you know who they are, we have written this chapter to help you boost them into the top-performing category.

Dozens of books have been written about sales coaching. It is not our intent to rehash in one chapter all of those best practices that make up effective sales coaching. This chapter is narrowly aimed at taking the ideas we've described in the rest of this book, and inculcating them among the coachable middle. As sales managers, we know that it's our job to improve the performance of our sales team. Simply telling a sales rep to think more strategically, or to sell smarter, is about as effective as a platoon leader telling his troops to go get the bad guys. It's the right idea in theory, but a little vague in practice. Unless you can help them understand *what* to do and *how* to do it, it will likely not get done (or not get done well).

Chuck Pfarrer was a commander in the elite U.S. Navy SEAL Team Six, whose members took down the world's most wanted man, Osama bin Laden. The preparation for this mission took months. All the members of SEAL Team Six had the best training; they were conditioned and ready for action. However, without developing a strategic plan, without discussing its payoffs and potential risks, and without rehearsing it, it's likely the results would have been significantly different.

We are willing to bet that your sales reps have the foundational skillset necessary to succeed on the job, or you probably would not have them on your team. It's your task as their manager to keep their skills sharp, to challenge their thinking, and to help them apply what they know in a more effective way. Without proper strategic direction, our reps can become complacent and lose their edge. At some point we've all seen our sales reps begin to make too many assumptions about what's happening inside their accounts. Our job is to challenge those assumptions and help our reps see the barriers or opportunities differently.

The members of U.S. Navy SEAL Team Six were ready for their strategic mission. They worked with their commanding officer to develop their strategy; they walked through all possible scenarios and devised plans to overcome any possible obstacle. As sales managers, we need to do the same with our reps—help them prepare for any possible scenario that may unfold when going after an opportunity.

In this chapter, we provide you with a simple, six-step strategic coaching process that will help your team build smarter opportunity plans, which in turn will help them win more business. The six simple steps are:

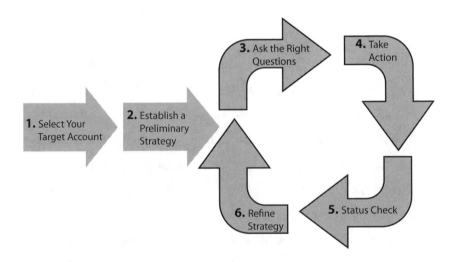

Step 1—Selecting Your Target: A military commander sets his sights on one or two specific targets, narrowing his scope. Why? Because he probably does not have the resources to help him focus on more than one or two targets at one time. So, just as military strategists understand the need to focus on the most crucial targets, successful sales strategists carefully select those few opportunities that are most important. They realize there is neither the time nor the resources to hit every available target. (This is why you will observe us visibly shuddering when we hear companies claim partnering relationships with nearly all their customers; not only is this not advisable, it's not even feasible.) If you want to improve your strategy coaching, a good place to begin is selecting the right accounts on which to focus your efforts. But how do you choose which opportunities to pursue?

We need to mention up front that this activity is no different from a customer's process in selecting a vendor. The first step may be to create a set of targeting criteria—choosing those things that are important in working with a customer. You may consider things like financial viability or credit worthiness. Of course, the overall revenue potential and profitability should be factors, as should the budget allotment your company receives in an account as compared to your competitor. How about *referenceability*? (That is, is this customer someone whose name you could drop on occasion to gain credibility with others?) You may also consider your current relationship status. Is a company more attractive if you are already doing some business with it? And what about its future growth potential?

After developing a list of targeting criteria, you should then prioritize them. What is most important and what is least important? This simple task can actually prove quite difficult and even somewhat arbitrary. For many sales reps, it is daunting, which is why your guidance will be invaluable. The ranking depends greatly on many factors, such as your market and your place in it, your strengths and weaknesses in the market, and your company's overall strategic objectives.

The third step in this process is comparing the prioritized list of selection criteria to the accounts in the territory. Who is most attractive and who is least, based on their alignment with the criteria?

Step A: Create Target Criteria

- Revenue Potential
- Budget Availability
- Perception of Your Company
- Early Adopter of New Technology
- Current Relationship

Step B: Prioritize the Criteria

1. Current Relationship
2. Budget Availability
3. Perception of Your Company
4. Early Adopter of New Technology
5. Revenue Potential

Step C: Compare Criteria to Your Accounts

- SLG's Pet Resort
- Poppy's Landscaping
- Aidan's Fabrics
- RKJ Auto
- KING Event Planning

Sales reps often believe that all of their prospects are equally attractive. We find this to be true whether the seller is a cock-eyed optimist or a jaundiced skeptic. One frequent trap is targeting an account simply because it meets one or two of the criteria. For example, sales reps left to their own devices often choose to target those customers with whom they have a good relationship. Unfortunately, this criterion alone rarely makes for a smart targeting strategy. Therefore, investing significant time to develop a comprehensive opportunity strategy based on one or two factors may be a poor use of resources.

To create value in this process, you have to gather meaningful information about the prospects and the market. It's difficult to provide strategic input if you don't know the targets very well. Developing a smart strategic plan also requires contributions from multiple people with varying perspectives. Working collectively will produce better results for your sales rep than if he worked on his own. And what's needed from these collaborators is not necessarily subject matter expertise, but something that might be called "subject matter skepticism."

The mistake of targeting accounts that meet only one or two criteria played out quite graphically for one of our clients, a global financial solutions provider. Terry, an area sales director, and his team had recently implemented a strategic opportunity planning process. Terry was excited about the new process and asked his sales team to begin applying it to "their highest revenue potential accounts." This was a reasonable request, and in some situations, maybe a smart request. Unfortunately for Terry, his plan didn't work as well as he had hoped.

Pat was one of Terry's sales reps. Pat wanted to apply the new opportunity planning process to a major manufacturer where he had been trying to get some traction, but without success. Pat, following Terry's directions, had selected the account because it had significant revenue potential. His top competitor owned the account, and had owned it for some time. But Pat had been steadily working to build relationships with some influential advocates. He was getting some signals that he might have a shot of getting his foot in the door.

So, Terry worked with Pat to develop a strategic plan for this target using the new process. Together, they established a number of action items and began to implement them. Pat's enthusiasm for the process and his confidence in his plan were high. However, 30 days into their plan, Pat learned that the customer had extended their contract with his top competitor. Pat's window of opportunity was closed. How did this happen? How could Pat not know that his competitor was in the midst of negotiating a contract extension with the customer?

Unfortunately, scenarios like this play out all too often. A sales rep targets an account, hours are put into developing a preliminary strategy, the rep invests time with the customer, information is swapped between the sales rep and the customer, but in the end...it was all for naught.

The opportunity vanishes like a mirage.

One of the most valuable contributions you can make as a sales manager is to play the role of "subject matter skeptic," to ask difficult, probing questions that test your sellers' assumptions and challenge their current thinking about their targeted accounts. It's a Cartesian account strategy: Question everything. Certainly, it's important for the seller and his chances of pursuing the right targets. But it can also be beneficial for you as you work through your own scarce resources. How many fool's errands can you pursue without compromising the very real, winnable opportunities before you?

Step 2—Establishing a Preliminary Strategy: Once the target account has been identified, it's critical to schedule time to develop or strengthen a strategy. However, prior to formally meeting with your sales rep, you should encourage her to develop a preliminary strategy on her own. What are her ideas? What is her preferred approach?

When SEAL Team Six began to develop their strategy to capture Osama bin Laden, a small group of people got together to first develop a preliminary strategy. The group included those who knew the situation best. Your sales reps should know best what's happening inside their target opportunities. They will have the best insights into what strategies may or may not work, and why. They should know who the key influencers are and how to maneuver through the account. Therefore, you should expect your rep to come to a formal strategic planning meeting with some initial ideas regarding what approaches may work best and potential barriers or traps. There is no such thing as a generic sales strategy. Each customer—and each opportunity—is unique. Capturing the business is not about *selecting* a strategy; it's about *formulating* a strategy. And formulating a winning strategy is all about having a comprehensive understanding of the customer.

Going back to our case study, Pat had some background information on his targeted customer, but didn't have enough information to determine if it was a smart target. If Pat had begun to develop a preliminary strategy, he may have figured out that he didn't have enough information, or would have learned about the possible contract extension sooner and thus selected another account.

Having your sales rep walk through the process of developing a preliminary strategy has two key benefits. First, it provides you, as her manager, some insights into what she knows and doesn't know about the opportunity. At a minimum, your sales rep should have an understanding of the business environment and the account's business objectives, as well as a good sense of the decision factors, who the key influencers are, and what the competitive landscape looks like.

A second benefit to having the sales rep establish a preliminary strategy is that it will provide you insights into which courses of action have worked well in this account—and which have not. It's difficult to develop a smart strategy if you don't have some of these basic insights. As we stated earlier, SEAL Team Six had some critical information about their target. For instance, they knew the layout and size of his compound, as well as its location. They knew the size and strength of his forces. They were familiar with his daily routines. With this information, they were able to assess the relative merits of competing strategies and develop an approach which had the highest likelihood of success.

Step 3—Asking the Right Questions: Top coaches in any field understand the importance of challenging the individuals on their teams, pushing them beyond what they thought they were capable of doing. People often excel when pushed outside of their comfort zones. The best coaches do not employ a one-size-fits-all methodology, but rather tailor their approach according to the individuals they are trying to push. The goal is to help their team break through mental and physical barriers in order to achieve success. In strategic opportunity planning, this often takes the form of asking questions that shake up reps' settled ideas about their accounts.

While working with a capital equipment manufacturer, we saw the dangers of using a one-size-fits-all plan for sales coaching. Lisa was one of the company's top sales managers and she managed seven reps. Lisa met with her team every Monday over the phone. She conducted one-on-one phone meetings with each sales rep to review the top accounts each was working on for the month. Lisa and the rep talked about an average of six to eight accounts in each call. These represented the reps' targeted accounts.

As part of our work with this client, we shadowed Lisa during her Monday meetings. The first one was with Kevin, a solid if unspectacular performer, who usually hit his quotas. Kevin had been with the company for two years.

Lisa began by getting a list of Kevin's top accounts. Starting at the top of the list, Lisa asked a series of questions about the account. Who was Kevin's main advocate? Who else did Kevin know? Who were his adversaries? What was Kevin selling? Why did the customer want it? What was the revenue potential? What stage was it in? When would it close? Did Kevin need any help from her? Kevin was able to answer the questions fairly quickly and effortlessly. Lisa then went onto the next account on the list.

This Q&A process played out pretty much the same way for all of Lisa's reps she met with that day. She asked virtually the same questions of each rep, and each rep supplied her with answers. We wondered if every Monday looked and sounded the same way, with the cast of characters changing ever so slightly. What we most wanted to know was how valuable the process was for the individuals involved. For Lisa, it was an all-day affair as she ploughed through each phone call.

It was also a significant investment of the reps' time. We wondered about the perceived return on that investment, as well as real returns, as measured by opportunities won.

In a candid moment, Lisa acknowledged that the reps resisted the Monday meetings, and she secretly loathed them. Her entire day was sucked dry, for one thing. "But I have to know what's going on in the field because my boss is asking me. And if I don't know what's going on, I run the risk of being caught out if a deal turns sideways. That is not pretty when it happens." Like the other managers with whom she worked, Lisa also felt that the information gathered from these weekly meetings, despite the reps' less-than-enthusiastic participation, was nonetheless valuable to the team.

For our client, the most alarming part of Lisa's revelation was that she was only one of five sales managers who conducted weekly meetings like these. Each manager followed a similar process. Extrapolated out, that was quite a bit of time spent reviewing accounts. We did not doubt that the other managers shared some of Lisa's reluctance to the meetings. On the other hand, even though they didn't enjoy them, the managers all felt they were helping their sales reps move their opportunities closer to fruition.

Here's where the story took a turn for the ironic. The sales teams hated the weekly meetings. The reps seemed to chafe at both the structure of the meetings and the content. One of the reps told us, "I hate these Monday meetings. They are almost always a waste of time. They insult my intelligence. And they do not really help me win business. The questions my manager asks me can be answered with a report from our CRM. Why waste my time with something our database can provide?"

While we wanted to commend our client for insisting that managers had regular and formal communication with their sales teams, we wondered if they knew how counterproductive the meetings actually were. At its simplest level, you could say this was a failure of their questioning model. Here's what we mean. Almost everyone involved in sales performance improvement will tell you that a question-based customer contact model is the way to sell. We have known since the days of Socrates that questions tend to be more persuasive than statements. This question-based approach is also effective in coaching.

However, not all questions are created equal (and not all of them are equally effective). In other words, contrary to what your teachers have told you, there actually *are* dumb questions.

If our client's sales managers had actually heard the frustration of their sales teams over the Monday meetings, there might have been some ruffled feathers and hurt feelings. Doubtless there would be some self-justifying and explaining. There might even be some managerial dismissiveness ("Well, you know salespeople; they think they know it all and always feel the need to complain about something"). But none of this confronts the truth about their broken process. We wanted to show them a better approach—but still a question-based approach.

The effectiveness of a question-based approach stems from two primary sources. The first is the process itself. Essentially, questions allow someone to persuade himself, which is significantly more effective than having to be persuaded by someone else. Once again, as the old saying goes, "If you say it, they can doubt it, but if they say it, it's true."

The second source of the approach's effectiveness stems from the questions themselves—the manner in which they are asked and what they are asking. It was in this second area where our client's sales managers were failing.

Presenting a position paper on why and how to ask good questions is beyond the scope of this book. But there are some "best practices" for questions that are worth exploring here and that will help you to be more effective in coaching your sales teams.

Lisa and her sales management peers took the right approach from a process standpoint, but they went awry in *how* they were seeking information. The first rule of good questioning is, "Never ask the obvious question that you can answer on your own." For instance, in selling it is unwise to ask a customer about his annual revenue when those numbers can be found in a publicly available source (like an annual report). Questions that can be answered without the input of the other party are best left unasked. And this is where our client's sales managers were stumbling. If they didn't already know the answers to the questions they were asking, they could access them as easily as the reps could.

In strategic opportunity planning, the job of the sales manager is not to play "stump the reps" but rather to challenge their assumptions and conclusions about what seems to be happening in their accounts and what they are planning to do about it. It is less "what" and more "so what," in other words. Coming up with the questions that challenge our reps' thinking requires planning. Just like we expect our sales reps to plan their questions before a sales call, top sales managers plan their questions prior to a strategic opportunity planning meeting. And just like in a sales call, we want to ask questions that cause the person to stop and think, to consider potential implications, and to draw inferences. Moreover, an effective questioning strategy goes deep before it goes wide. That is, effective sales managers dig deeper on an issue before moving on.

The process our client's sales managers were using looked more like a perfunctory interrogation. It had a rhythm. And any rhythm repeated over time becomes monotonous. An alternative approach is to listen to the answer to the first question, and follow it up with questions based specifically on that answer.

After working with Lisa and her peers on a more effective questioning approach, we again shadowed them during their Monday calls. Here is a partial transcript of how the conversation played out between Lisa and Kevin, one of her reps.

> *Lisa: Who do you believe is your top advocate in this account?*
>
> *Kevin: I believe it's Dr. Kelley.*
>
> *Lisa: What's been said or done to make you believe Dr. Kelley is an advocate?*
>
> *Kevin: He has always accepted my meetings and been forthcoming with information.*
>
> *Lisa: Does he provide your competitor with the same access and information?*
>
> *Kevin: I'm not really sure.*
>
> *Lisa: What does Dr. Kelley think about our competitor?*
>
> *Kevin: I'm not really sure.*
>
> *Lisa: How can we find out and be sure he is being honest with us?*

Kevin: I guess I could ask him his opinion about our competitor and try to find out what he likes best and least about them.

Lisa: That would definitely be helpful. Do you know who our competitors' advocates might be?

Kevin: Um, I'm not sure.

Lisa: How can we find out? And once we have that insight what might be your next step in neutralizing our competitor's advocates?

The types of questions that Lisa is asking Kevin are questions that Kevin hasn't given any consideration to and will help him avoid any painful surprises in the end. As stated earlier, these types of questions require some time to prepare. To help you in this process we are providing you a few sample questions that you might find useful. These questions are broken down by the critical elements found in a smart strategic opportunity plan.

These questions should not be used randomly or haphazardly. They should be used only when preparing for a high impact strategic opportunity planning meeting about one of your targeted accounts.

Critical Buying Factors

1. What are the key steps in this customer's buying process? Where is this customer in their buying process?

2. What concerns you most about the customer's buying factors, and what is your strategy to alleviate these concerns?

3. What assumptions might you have made regarding these buying factors? How can you validate your assumptions?

4. If you are late in the process, how will you catch up? If you are early, can you do anything to make it move more quickly?

5. What leads you to believe this is a long decision process?

6. What's driving the sense of urgency for this account?

7. Do we need to have 100 percent consensus to drive a decision?

8. Is there anything we can do to slow down the buying process?

9. Who do you believe is driving this buying process?

10. Outside of economics, what else do you think we need to find out about this buying process? Who do you think we could ask to better understand this?

Managing Key Players

1. Who have you identified as your advocates and adversaries?

2. What has been said or done to have you believe they are your advocate or adversary?

3. What business issues are they trying to solve?

4. What is your strategy to leverage your advocates?

5. Who are your competitors' advocates?

6. What is your strategy to win support from those who are adversaries? What are the barriers that could prevent that from happening?

7. What are some things that the adversaries value? How can we influence those things?

8. Who do you believe is the ultimate decision maker? What have you done to gain commitment from that person?

9. Have you spoken with any of your colleagues in other divisions to understand the depth of this initiative?

10. Is there anyone external to the customer that we can leverage to help us win this opportunity?

Knowing Your Environment

1. Which market trends are having the greatest impact on this customer? How will it affect our sales efforts?

2. What new initiatives has this account taken to leverage or combat these new trends?

3. Which players inside the account are the key stakeholders for this new initiative?

4. What responsibility do these stakeholders have to help their company take advantage of or combat the trends in the market?

5. What are specific actions we can take to help these stakeholders look like heroes?

6. What actions might the competition take that could hurt our efforts inside this account?

7. Is there anything going on inside our company that might affect this opportunity?

Understanding the Competitive Landscape

1. What are the customer's selection criteria?

2. Who have you spoken to validate the selection criteria?

3. If there are multiple decision makers, do they all agree on the same selection criteria? Whose selection criteria matter most and why?

4. How does the customer perceive our ability to meet their needs?

5. Who is our competition in this opportunity?

6. What selection criteria are strengths of our competitors? What is your strategy to strengthen our position in these areas?

7. What barriers could you run into when trying to strengthen our position?

8. Is there a specific "play" that the competitors could try (and that we haven't thought of)?

9. How does your solution help the customer meet his goal?

10. How else do you see us bringing value to this customer?

There is not enough time or necessity to participate in this kind of Q&A for every single account owned by your sales reps. For this reason, we strongly encourage you to help your reps target the right accounts.

Step 4—Taking Action—Moving in for the Attack: Though there were some unfortunate and terribly sad circumstances that happened during the execution of Navy SEAL Team Six's strategy to capture Osama bin Laden, none of them were unanticipated. The planners had carefully considered multiple contingencies the way a chess master plays an entire round out mentally before doing it physically. SEAL Team Six rehearsed as many possible scenarios as could be imagined prior to executing their strategy. Every person knew his role in the strategy and what to do in each scenario.

In selling, the same sort of rigorous contingency planning just makes sense. Playing out the many "what if" scenarios, thinking through roles, responsibilities, and responses, and rehearsing are all essential elements of executing a strategy effectively. Too often sales managers assume their sales rep knows what to do and how to do it. This assumption causes many great sales strategies to go to waste. We have seen some very smart sales strategies developed over the years, but unfortunately, they were poorly executed, and thus never achieved the results that were expected. Sales managers also often fail to realize they also have a role in executing the sales strategy, even if it does not involve leading from the front. It could be interacting with customers, or possibly, it could be making way for something to happen inside their own organizations.

The number one way to avoid these common traps is to write out the plan of attack. Top sales managers today realize that it's a good idea to write down what, who, and when. What needs to be done to strengthen our position? Who is responsible for making it happen? When is it going to be done?

Coming back to our client's case, after Lisa understood the importance of asking questions that challenged her reps' thinking, she found another problem. The questions she asked often revealed how much her team did not know. After every meeting, the sales reps walked away with tasks to complete and information to gather before the next meeting.

So we also helped Lisa realize that this task list deserved some prioritization. For example, she knew that Kevin couldn't meet with his adversary until he got access to a few top references in his territory that would agree to speak on his behalf. She also realized that she had to twist a few arms inside her own company to make some things happen. Taking time to prioritize the action items and assigning responsibility for each helped Lisa ensure that they were completed.

Establishing a well-thought-out action plan also allows for smart and timely follow-up. Often the agenda for your next meeting with your rep is already established. It's all about following up on the action items you both agreed were critical to the strategic plan.

Step 5—Status Check: Stacy was a top performer working as an executive recruiter. He was responsible for acquiring and managing his company's top 25 accounts. He had great relationships with all of his customers. His account base included companies like Goldman Sachs, Moody's, NASDAQ, and others in the financial market. He had been given a new opportunity when one of the executives he placed five years ago at VISA accepted a new job offer at American Express. Stacy had been trying to get into American Express for the past two years and hadn't had any luck. He knew this was the break he was looking for. His experience told him that he needed to be smart and develop a strategy to effectively leverage his contact. Stacy sat down with his management team to discuss how to best leverage his relationship to get his foot in the door at American Express. He and his management team developed a solid strategy. They discussed the potential traps and how to avoid them or overcome them should they arise. He rehearsed his plan and was ready to take action. A week later Stacy met with his management team to review how well the strategy worked. Stacy told them that although he didn't achieve the main objective, he was able to gain some new information that was critical going forward. He had learned who the key influencers were in the decision for hiring executive recruiters. He had also learned that American Express was preparing to expand into the fleet fuel card business and was expecting to hire seven new executives in the next 90 days to lead this new business unit. With this new information, Stacy and his management team knew they had a real opportunity to help American Express and that winning their business would require an updated strategy.

We often find that sales managers believe that once they have helped develop an opportunity strategy their work is done. They are then unpleasantly surprised when critical circumstances in the account change or the sales rep falls short of expectations when executing the strategy. To prevent this, sales managers must do a status check on the unfolding of the strategic plan and examine how new developments or information affect it.

In some cases when a strategy isn't able to be fully executed, it could be because of factors outside the rep's control. Think about a time when you established a solid strategy for helping your sales rep gain access to the C-suite. The two of you sat down to understand who all of the key influencers were and you developed a strategy to leverage your advocates to get you access to the C-suite. You discussed the potential barriers you might run into along the way and you even rehearsed how to overcome those potential barriers. Yet, there was one factor that no one could have expected, which prevented your strategy from being fully executed. For reasons like this, it's critical to meet with your sales reps for a status check.

Without a status check it's difficult to determine if the strategy was faulty or if the execution was poor. We all want to believe our top performers know how to execute a strategy that was jointly developed. Unfortunately, even top performers sometimes fall short of our expectations when it comes to strategy execution. Therefore, this step allows managers to learn what went well and what didn't go well. It is through this dialog that an existing strategy can be refined.

Step 6—Refining Your Strategy: In every strategic opportunity there are events happening that possibly could change your course of action. Some of these events could be based upon how, what, or when we are selling into any given account. According to Newton's third law, which states that every action has equal reaction in the opposite direction, after every client interaction there will most likely be a new set of action steps. As sales managers we need to remember that this often will require refining the strategy. Assuming your sales rep will come up with the correct refined strategy on their own is often a dangerous assumption. Factors like new key players, new competitors, or new strategic direction of the company are influential enough upon the customer's buying decision that a new look at the existing strategy is warranted.

To be effective at refining a strategy requires sales manager to know what questions to ask. As we demonstrated earlier in this chapter, asking questions that merely assess basic, easily-retrievable information on the account doesn't help formulate new strategic ideas. It's imperative that we go back to asking those strategic coaching questions that force our sales reps back on their heels and cause them to think about the situation differently.

Going back to our story with Lisa and Kevin, the questions Lisa was asking Kevin forced him to think about critical factors in his account that he hadn't given consideration to in the past. When new factors are brought into the strategic opportunity discussion, there are often significant implications that can play to our advantage or disadvantage. Therefore, it's necessary to keep refining your strategy to be sure you're always moving the sales opportunity forward.

Chapter 8 Summary

Successful strategic sales coaching requires consistency and accountability. If you elect to adopt a consistent strategic opportunity planning process, you must hold your team accountable for following that process. For example, when reviewing the pipeline process, look at the milestones within each pipeline stage and ask yourself what coaching questions you should ask to challenge your reps' thinking about them. The more your reps are held accountable for targeting the right accounts and developing a smart preliminary strategy, the more likely it is that your strategy meetings will be productive. And if you are consistent in your style of questioning—challenging your reps' thinking, helping them think creatively—your reps will come better prepared to these meetings.

About the Authors

Steve Gielda

For more than 20 years, Steve has been helping companies throughout the world improve their sales performance and meet their business goals. Steve is a salesperson to the core—he loves working with clients, understanding their needs, and helping them improve their business outcomes.

Steve started his career at Lanier Worldwide, pounding the pavement and knocking on doors. His success as a salesperson and his desire to take on leadership roles allowed Steve to move into the positions of District Manager and Region Sales Director. Steve's success comes from his persistence and willingness to forge strong client relationships. He understands the importance of building smart sales strategies that are linked to driving his clients' business goals. Steve began his career in sales training in 1997 when he joined Huthwaite, Inc. Steve later established his own practice as partner with the Advantage Performance Group, then later as a principal with Sales Momentum. In 2010, Steve and Kevin joined together to form Ignite Selling, Inc.

Kevin Jones

For more than 15 years, Kevin has been designing and delivering training solutions that impact people's lives. Kevin's goal is to create a learning environment where participants can thrive and where lessons learned can be translated to the field. Kevin has worked in finance, sales, and sales training. It was in sales training that Kevin found his true passion—developing people.

Kevin received a bachelor's degree in business from North Carolina State University, and a master's in business administration from the Kenan-Flagler Business School at the University of North Carolina at Chapel Hill. Kevin uses his academic exposure and real-world experience to develop training solutions that drive business results. Kevin's work has enabled him to influence hundreds of companies in more than 30 countries worldwide.

About Ignite Selling, Inc.

The founders of Ignite Selling, Inc. have worked in the sales performance improvement business for more than 15 years. We have collectively interacted with the sales forces of more than 250 companies worldwide. We've helped companies in multiple industries, including healthcare, distribution, publishing, automotive, and manufacturing—just to name a few. In our experiences, we have seen training initiatives both succeed and fail to produce the desired results. What makes us different from other sales training consultancies isn't our experience—lots of training companies have worked in the business a long time and across a broad base of companies. It also isn't the fact that we teach proven best practices in selling behaviors or strategy development—most consultants do this. What makes Ignite Selling, Inc. different is *how* we build your solution.

Every company has goals it wants to achieve. And the sales team plays a critical role in helping the company achieve those goals. Most sales training companies build their programs regardless of their customer's goals—because they are focused only on selling behaviors. We start by understanding the goals our customer is trying to achieve, and establish what the sales team needs to do in order for it to help accomplish those goals. Once we know what the sales team needs to do, we build our program to help them do it—simple! If something isn't important or won't actively help the sales team achieve your goals, then we don't teach it. If it is critical to your success, then we teach it and practice it to mastery. No two programs are alike, because no two companies' goals are identical. Ignite Selling, Inc. builds the bridge between classroom lessons and real-world success and that's what sets us apart.

To contact Ignite Selling, Inc. please call 703.266.7667 or email sales@igniteselling.com.

Sales Simulations that Inspire